THE
GIANT

Book of
BIBLE
FINGERPLAYS
for Preschoolers
BY AMY HOUTS

Loveland, Colorado
group.com

Group resources really work!

This Group resource incorporates our R.E.A.L. approach to ministry. It reinforces a growing friendship with Jesus, encourages long-term learning, and results in life transformation, because it's

Relational
Learner-to-learner interaction enhances learning and builds Christian friendships.

Experiential
What learners experience through discussion and action sticks with them up to 9 times longer than what they simply hear or read.

Applicable
The aim of Christian education is to equip learners to be both hearers and doers of God's Word.

Learner-based
Learners understand and retain more when the learning process takes into consideration how they learn best.

The Giant Book of Bible Fingerplays for Preschoolers

Visit our website: group.com

CREDITS
Author: Amy Houts
Chief Creative Officer: Joani Schultz
Executive Editor: Christine Yount Jones
Managing Editor: Jennifer Hooks
Editor: Ann Diaz
Cover Illustration: James Talbot
Cover Design: James Talbot
Production Artist: Amber Gomez Balanzar
Art Director: RoseAnne Sather

ISBN 978-1-4707-4478-6

10 9 8 7 6 5 4 3 2 1   26 25 24 23 22 21 20 19 18 17

Printed in the United States of America.

Contents

OLD TESTAMENT

Contents *continued*

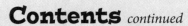

NEW TESTAMENT

THE **GIANT** BOOK OF BIBLE FINGERPLAYS FOR PRESCHOOLERS

Introduction

Welcome to The Giant Book of Bible Fingerplays for Preschoolers!

The Giant Book of Bible Fingerplays for Preschoolers gets children actively involved in telling Bible events that shape God's great story. No supplies are needed—just this book! Each page features a Bible verse and passage to read, along with a Bible fingerplay that preschoolers can say and act out with you. What better way for young children to learn about the Bible? Imagine a lesson time with listening, speaking, and action. Sounds like fun!

THIS BOOK:

• teaches Bible passages on an age-appropriate level
• features a key Bible verse from each passage
• includes 101 fingerplays

What Is a Fingerplay?

A fingerplay is a short verse, poem, or rhyme where hand and body movements act out the words being said. Young children enjoy actively engaging in telling the passage along with you. Acting out the passage helps children remember the details while keeping them interested and having fun!

FINGERPLAYS IN THIS BOOK:

• teach Bible passages
• are easy to learn and remember
• are fun, fast attention-getters
• can be sung to the tune *Frère Jacques*
• contain short versions of Bible passages from the Old and New Testaments

How to Use This Book

Active children like to be involved in the Bible passages you read and teach. This book has three components for each activity: an easy-to-understand telling of the Bible passage, a related Bible verse, and a fun fingerplay. Each component plays a part in helping children learn about the Bible in an engaging way. Use this book with one child or with a group of children.

First, read children the Bible verse. When you read the Bible verse, clap once for each syllable; then repeat. This helps children learn the verse by heart. For example, in the verse "And God saw that it was good," all the words have one syllable. Clap once as you say each word, and encourage children to clap with you. Each dot equals one clap.

Let's try it:

•   •   •   •   •   •   •

And God saw that it was good.

In the verse "An angel said to Mary, 'The Lord is with you,'" some of the words have one syllable and some have two. Clap once for the one-syllable words, and clap twice for the two-syllable words. Each dot equals one clap. Let's try it:

•   • •   • • •   •   • •   •   •

An angel said to Mary, "The Lord is with you."

Next, read aloud the simplified Bible passage. Want to find the full passage and verse in the Bible? See the Bible reference listed under the passage title. Once you've read the Bible verse and Bible passage, act out the fingerplay.

Reading these three components *(verse, passage, fingerplay)* helps children learn and understand the passage. You can read these components separately, too. Read and repeat the verse to practice memorization. Focus on the Bible passage, saving the verse and fingerplay for another time. If you want to get everyone's attention, act out a fingerplay.

How Do You Act Out a Fingerplay?

Fingerplays are fun and easy! Teach them line by line, speaking the words as you do the actions in parentheses.

For example, in the first fingerplay, *Creation*, say the words "God created" while doing the action: "*(curve fingers, hands apart to form a ball)*." Children should repeat the words and mimic your actions. Then go to the second line, saying "All the heavens" while doing the action: "*(point up)*." Continue until you complete the verse. Each fingerplay has a total of eight lines. If children are having trouble or are reluctant to follow, you can repeat the verse and action again, or just go on. They will get the hang of it.

Perform each of the 101 fingerplays in this book the same way, saying the words and performing the actions. You'll be surprised at how children will be able to memorize and act out the Bible passage fingerplays! They might even begin to say them on their own without any prompting from you.

To make it even easier, you can sing the fingerplays. Each one can be sung to the tune of the French nursery rhyme "Frère Jacques." Do you remember this nursery rhyme? Here are the words, as translated in English:

Are you sleeping?

Are you sleeping?

Brother John,

Brother John?

Morning bells are ringing.

Morning bells are ringing.

Ding, ding, dong.

Ding, ding, dong.

The Giant Book of Bible Fingerplays for Preschoolers is more than fun—using it will help children grow and develop. Children will gain knowledge about Bible events and truths. Children will learn to speak new words, which helps with language development and pre-reading skills. Saying and acting out these passages will help children develop fine motor control by using the small muscles in their fingers and mouths. Knowledge, language development, pre-reading skills, and fine motor control are all important ways young children grow and develop.

My hope is that this book will introduce your child or Sunday school class to the Bible, and begin a lifelong journey and love of Bible reading.

—Amy Houts, author

 **Amy Houts** *taught preschool at Head Start and as a graduate assistant in the early childhood department at Northwest Missouri State University. She is an award-winning author of over 60 children's books and numerous articles and poetry. Amy and her husband attend the First United Methodist Church in Maryville, Missouri, where Amy has been in involved in Sunday school, vacation Bible school, Bible study, and committee work for many years. They have two grown daughters and twin grandsons.*

Creation

Genesis 1-2

God made the earth and the heavens in six days.

God said: "Let there be light." And God saw it was good.

God said: "Let the waters separate." And God saw it was good.

God said, "Let fish swim in the water and birds fly in the sky." And God saw it was good.

God said, "Let there be animals." And God saw it was good.

God said, "Let there be man and woman." And God saw it was *very* good.

On the seventh day, God rested from his work.

Fingerplay

God created (*curve fingers, hands apart to form a ball*)

All the heavens (*point up*)

And the earth (*point down*)

In six days. (*hold up six fingers*)

Animals and insects, (*wave hands like flying*)

First man and then woman. (*hold up one finger, then two*)

Seventh day: (*hold up seven fingers*)

Rest, rest, rest. (*palms together, rest cheek on hands*)

God Said

Genesis 2-3

BIBLE VERSE

"The Lord God made all kinds of trees grow." (Genesis 2:9)

God planted a garden. The plants grew. Trees grew.

"See the garden?" God said to Adam. "You can eat of any tree in the garden."

In the middle of the garden was a special tree.

"See that tree?" God said to Adam. "Do not eat fruit from that tree."

God created a woman for Adam.

"See the garden?" God said to the woman. "You can eat of any tree in the garden."

Then he pointed to the special tree.

"See that tree?" God said to the woman. "Do not eat fruit from that tree."

Fingerplay

"See the garden, (extend arms, palms up)

Lovely garden (hands clasped)

I have made?" (point to self)

Said the Lord. (point up)

"Do not eat the fruit of (shake head no)

This tree in the garden (wag pointer finger)

I command," (point to self)

Said the Lord. (point up)

Eve Ate the Apple

Genesis 3

"Can you eat the fruit of any tree?" a snake asked the woman.
"Not that tree," said the woman. "Not the tree in the middle of the garden."
The snake hissed: "If you do, you will be like God."
"If I do, I will be like God," said the woman.
So the woman picked the fruit. She took a bite.
Then she gave the fruit to Adam. Adam took a bite.
Then they were afraid.

Fingerplay

The snake told her *(cup hands near mouth)*

To be like God, *(point up)*

"Eat the fruit." *(hand to mouth)*

So she did. *(hand to mouth)*

Then she said to Adam, *(cup hands near mouth)*

"Adam, would you like some?" *(pretend to hold apple)*

"Yes, I would," *(nod head yes)*

Adam said. *(hand to mouth)*

Leaving the Garden

Genesis 3

Adam and the woman hid from God behind a tree. "Where are you?" asked God.

"I was afraid," said Adam. "So I hid."

"Why?" asked God. "Did you eat fruit from the tree in the middle of the garden?"

"The woman gave me the fruit," said Adam. "So I ate it."

"The snake lied to me," said the woman. "So I ate it."

God was angry, and he was disappointed.

"You must leave the garden," said God.

Adam named his wife Eve.

God made clothing for Adam and Eve. Then they left the Garden of Eden.

BIBLE VERSE

"So the Lord God banished him from the Garden of Eden." (Genesis 3:23)

Fingerplay

God cared so much; *(point up; then hug self)*

God cared so much *(point up; hug self)*

For Adam *(extend one arm, palm up)*

And for Eve. *(extend other arm, palm up)*

But God had to tell them, *(point up; then cup hands near mouth)*

"You must leave the garden." *(push air, palm outward)*

Adam left. *(walk in place)*

So did Eve. *(walk in place)*

Cain and Abel

Genesis 3–4

Eve would be the mother of all living things.
Eve gave birth to a baby boy. They named him Cain.
"The Lord helped me to have a baby!" said Eve.
For the first time, Eve was a mother. For the first time, Adam was a father.
Later, Eve gave birth to another baby boy. They named him Abel.
Cain was the older brother. Abel was the younger brother.

Fingerplay

Eve and Adam *(extend one arm, palm up, then the other)*

Had a baby *(clasp elbows, as if holding a baby)*

They called Cain; *(pretend to rock a baby)*

They called Cain. *(rock and look at baby)*

Eve wanted another *(clasp hands together, pleading)*

And they named him Abel. *(pretend to rock a baby)*

Two fine boys, *(extend one arm, palm up, then other)*

Two fine boys. *(hold up two fingers)*

Shepherd and Farmer

Genesis 4

Even though Cain and Abel were brothers, they were very different.
Cain liked to grow plants. He was a farmer.
Abel liked to herd sheep. He was a shepherd.
Cain worked in the dirt. Abel worked in the field.
Cain brought the Lord some vegetables as an offering.
Abel brought the Lord his best lambs as an offering.
God liked Abel's offering. God did not like Cain's offering.
Cain was angry. He was sad that God did not like his offering.

BIBLE VERSE

"The Lord looked with favor on Abel and his offering." (Genesis 4:4)

Fingerplay

Cain and Abel *(extend one arm, palm up, then the other)*

Helped their parents *(nod head yes)*

With the fields *(cup hand; thumb and pointer hold seed; pretend to plant)*

And the flocks. *(sweep finger in front of you, pointing to sheep)*

Abel was a shepherd, *(one hand out, palm up)*

And Cain was a farmer. *(other hand out, palm up)*

See the sheep. *(sweep finger in front of you)*

See the fields. *(cup hand; thumb and pointer hold seed; pretend to plant)*

Noah and the Ark

Genesis 6-9

God saw that Noah was a good man. "Build an ark," God said.

So Noah built a big boat called an ark. "Take two of every animal on the ark," God said.

So Noah took two of every animal on his ark. "I will send rain for 40 days," God said.

There was so much rain, the earth was flooded with water.

Noah and his family and the animals were safe on the ark.

Noah watched it rain for 40 days. They lived on the ark for many more days.

Then Noah sent a dove to find dry land. The dove flew back with an olive leaf.

Noah knew the olive leaf was from a tree growing on dry land.

Soon, Noah and his family and the animals left the ark to live on the land.

God sent a rainbow as a symbol of his promise never to flood the earth again.

Fingerplay

It was raining; *(fingers flutter down with "rain")*

It was storming. *(bend knees; shoulders up; fists near chin)*

Rain, rain, rain. *(arms across chest, head down)*

Wet, wet, wet! *(pretend to shake water off of hands)*

Noah built a big boat. *(hands wide apart, palms inward)*

He called all the animals *(cup hands near mouth)*

Two by two, *(hold up two fingers)*

Two by two. *(two fingers walking on opposite hand, palm up)*

Tower of Babel

Genesis 11

Long ago, everyone in the world spoke the same language. They all understood each other.

"Let's build a tower," the people said. "Let's build a city.

"Let's build a tower in the city up to the heavens!"

God came down to see the city. God came down to see the tower.

God did not like what he saw. The city and the tower were for people, not for God.

So God made the people speak different languages.

God scattered people all over the earth. Then they stopped building the city. They stopped building the tower.

Fingerplay

Build a tower; *(pretend to build with blocks)*

Build a tower *(make the tower higher)*

To the sky *(point to sky)*

To reach God. *(stand on tiptoes with arms extended)*

I don't understand you. *(shake head no)*

Tell me what you're saying. *(hand to ear)*

Go away! *(push air with hands, palms outward)*

Travel far. *(walk in place)*

God Told Abram

Genesis 15

"**W**hat can you give me, Lord?" asked Abram. "I have no children. I have no heirs. Who will I give my land to?"

"You will have a son," said God. "Look up at the stars and count them. That's how many heirs you will have."

God made promises to Abram.

"I will give your son and all who come after you the land from the river of Egypt to the great river, the Euphrates."

Then Abram was happy.

Fingerplay

God told Abram; *(hand by mouth)*

God told Abram: *(hand to mouth, whisper this time)*

Promises! *(hands clasped)*

Promises! *(hands clasped, look up)*

I will give you much land *(palms upward)*

And many descendants. *(extend hands outward and to the side)*

Travel near, *(walk in place to the left)*

Travel far. *(walk in place to the right)*

Lot's Wife

Genesis 19

BIBLE VERSE

"But Lot's wife looked back."
(Genesis 19:26)

God was angry with the city of Sodom. The people did not honor God.
The Lord sent two angels to Sodom.
A man named Lot fed the angels and gave them a place to sleep.
The angels told Lot to take his family and leave Sodom.
"God has sent us to destroy the city," the angels said. "Hurry! Take your wife and daughters."
The angels held the hands of Lot, his wife, and their two daughters.
The angels led Lot's family out of the city.
"Don't look back," the angels said.
When Lot reached the city of Zoar, the Lord rained fire upon Sodom.
But Lot's wife looked back, and she turned into a pillar of salt.

Fingerplay

Do not look back. *(cup hands near mouth as if shouting)*

Do not look back. *(shake head no)*

Run away! *(two fingers running, on opposite hand, palm upward)*

Run away! *(two fingers running, on opposite hand, palm upward)*

Lot's wife stopped and looked back. *(look back)*

Now she is a statue *(freeze in place)*

Made of salt, *(pound one palm with fist)*

Made of salt. *(pound the other palm with fist)*

Sarah Laughed

Genesis 17 and 21

BIBLE VERSE

"Sarah said, 'God has brought me laughter!'" (Genesis 21:6)

God changed Abram's name to Abraham.
God changed Sarai's name to Sarah.
The new names showed their lives were changing, too.
"I will bless Sarah and give her a son," God told Abraham.
"She will be the mother of all nations."
God was gracious to Sarah. She became pregnant even though she was 90 years old.
"Everyone will laugh with me!" said Sarah.

Fingerplay

Where is Sarah? *(hand above eyes, palm downward)*

She is laughing. *(hand on belly)*

Ha, ha, ha! *(cup hands near mouth, then outward with each "ha")*

What she heard. *(hand on ear)*

She will have a baby *(clasp elbows and rock baby)*

Even though she's older. *(shrug shoulders, palms up)*

Sarah said, *(extend arms and look up)*

"Thank you, God!" *(jump and clap for joy)*

Sarah's Baby

Genesis 17 and 21

Sarah and Abraham had waited so long for a baby.
Even though Abraham was 100 years old, God kept his promise.
Even though Sarah was 90 years old, God kept his promise.
Sarah gave birth to a son.
"God has made me happy!" said Sarah.
"I gave Abraham a son in his old age."
Abraham named his son Isaac. Isaac means "he laughs."

BIBLE VERSE

"The Lord did for Sarah what he had promised." (Genesis 21:1)

Fingerplay

Sarah waited *(both hands on tummy)*

For a baby. *(clasp elbows to hold baby)*

Then she laughed! *(cup hands near mouth, then outward)*

It's a boy. *(clasp elbows and rock baby)*

But what shall his name be? *(fist under chin, look up as if thinking)*

His name shall be Isaac. *(clap twice)*

Isaac means *(nod head yes)*

"He who laughs!" *(cup hands near mouth, then outward)*

Isaac and Rebekah

Genesis 24

Isaac grew up. Abraham asked his servant to choose a wife for Isaac.
The servant took 10 camels loaded with good things from Abraham.
He traveled close to the town of Nahor, stopping by a well.
The servant asked God for help in finding a wife for Isaac. He saw a girl.
"Let this girl be the one you have chosen," he prayed. "If I ask her for a drink, she will give a me drink. She will give water to my camels even if I don't ask."
The servant asked the girl, "May I have a drink?"
"Yes, please drink," said girl, offering him water from her jar.
 "I will give water to your camels," she said, even though the servant didn't ask.
She poured water into a trough for the camels to drink.
The servant asked her name. "I am Rebekah, the daughter of Bethuel," she said.
The servant praised God because Abraham knew Rebekah's family.
Rebekah went with the servant to marry Isaac.

Fingerplay

"May I have a (*extend hand, then point to self*)

Drink of water (*hand in fist; pretend to drink*)

From the well?" (*pretend to pull rope up from well*)

"Yes, you may." (*nod head yes*)

Will you marry Isaac? (*kneel down; clasp hands*)

I am Isaac's servant. (*point to self*)

Let me think; (*point to head*)

Yes, I will. (*clasp hands; nod head yes*)

Isaac's Prayer

Genesis 25

When Isaac was 40 years old, he married Rebekah.
They wanted to have a child.
They waited and waited, but Rebekah did not get pregnant.
So Isaac prayed to God to give them a child.
Then Rebekah became pregnant with twins.
The twins fought with each other before they were born.
Rebekah gave birth to twin boys. The first baby born had red skin and lots of hair, so they named him Esau. Esau means "red."
The second baby born was holding onto the heel of Esau's foot.
They named him Jacob. Jacob means "he grasps the heel."

Fingerplay

Isaac prayed to *(hands in prayer)*

Have a baby. *(clasp elbows as if holding a baby)*

They had twins, *(hold up two fingers)*

Two twin boys. *(bend elbows as if holding two babies)*

The firstborn was Esau; *(hold up one finger)*

Second born was Jacob. *(hold up two fingers)*

Baby boys, *(bend elbows as if holding two babies)*

Baby boys! *(sway back and forth holding babies)*

Esau and Jacob

Genesis 25

BIBLE VERSE

Jacob said, "First sell me your birthright." (Genesis 25:31)

Esau and Jacob grew up. They were twin brothers, but they were different.

Esau liked to hunt with a bow and arrow. Jacob liked to stay near the tents where they lived.

Their father, Isaac, loved Esau. Their mother, Rebekah, loved Jacob.

Esau was born first. Jacob was born second. Being born first was an honor.

One day Esau was very hungry when he came back from hunting.

Jacob was cooking lentil stew.

"Give me some stew," said Esau. "I'm starving!"

"I will trade you stew for your birthright," said Jacob. "Say I am the first born."

"You are the first born," said Esau.

Jacob gave Esau some stew. Now Jacob had the honor of being firstborn.

Fingerplay

Esau hunted. *(pretend to shoot a bow and arrow)*

Jacob stayed home *(point to floor)*

In their tents, *(fingertips together as in rooftop)*

In their tents. *(fingertips together over head in rooftop)*

They were very different, *(walk backward a few steps)*

Very different brothers. *(walk forward a few steps)*

One went out; *(point to door)*

One stayed home. *(point to floor)*

Jacob's Blessing

Genesis 27

When Isaac was old and could not see, he asked Esau to make him some food.

"I want to give you my blessing before I die," said Isaac.

Rebekah heard what Isaac had said and told Jacob. She wanted Jacob to receive the blessing.

So Rebekah made food for Jacob to bring to his father.

"Esau is hairy and I am not," said Jacob. "If my father touches me, he will know I am not Esau. Then he will not bless me."

So Rebekah dressed Jacob in Esau's clothing. She covered Jacob's hands and neck with goatskin.

Jacob went to his father. Isaac touched Jacob's hands and smelled his clothes. Jacob felt and smelled like Esau, so he received the blessing. Jacob gave Isaac food and bread.

Then Esau came back, and he was angry because Jacob had taken his blessing.

BIBLE VERSE

"May those who bless you be blessed," said Isaac. (Genesis 27:29)

Fingerplay

Jacob asked his (kneel; bow head)

Father's blessing: (hands in prayer)

"Please bless me. (point to self)

Please bless me." (point to self)

Esau didn't like that (shake head no)

Jacob had the blessing. (cross arms as if angry)

Esau said, (hands clasped, pleading)

"Please bless me!" (point to self)

Jacob's Ladder

Genesis 28

BIBLE VERSE

"I am with you,"
said the Lord.
(Genesis 28:15)

On his journey to Harran, Jacob stopped to sleep.

He put a stone under his head for a pillow.

He had a dream about a tall ladder.

The ladder went from the ground up to heaven.

Angels climbed up and down the ladder in between heaven and earth.

Above the ladder stood the Lord.

"I am the God of your father," the Lord said.

"I give you and all who come after you this land. All people will be blessed by you. I will watch over you."

Jacob woke up. "Awesome!" said Jacob. "God is in this place."

Fingerplay

Jacob rested *(palms together, cheek resting on hands)*

On a pillow *(curve fingers, hands apart, to form a ball)*

Made of stone *(hit fist in palm)*

On the ground. *(point to floor)*

Jacob saw a ladder *(hands climb ladder rungs)*

Going up to heaven *(point up)*

In his dream, *(point to head)*

In his dream. *(palms together, cheek resting on hands)*

Jacob and Rachel

Genesis 29

Jacob traveled to where his Uncle Laban lived.

There he met Laban's younger daughter, Rachel.

Jacob fell in love with Rachel. "I will work for seven years to marry Rachel," said Jacob.

So Jacob worked for seven years.

Rachel had an older sister, Leah. Laban tricked Jacob into marrying Leah.

"I cannot let you marry my younger daughter," said Laban, "until the older one is married. In a week, you can marry Rachel, too. But you must work another seven years."

In a week, Jacob married Rachel. Then he worked for Laban another seven years.

Fingerplay

Jacob worked for *(put one hand on hip)*

Uncle Laban. *(put other hand on hip)*

He worked hard, *(use back of one hand to wipe brow)*

Very hard. *(use back of other hand to wipe brow)*

"I have served you long years. *(point to self)*

May I marry Rachel?" *(kneel, hands clasped)*

"No, no, no. *(shake head no)*

Work some more." *(shake pointer finger)*

Joseph's Coat

Genesis 37

BIBLE VERSE

"He made an ornate robe for him."
(Genesis 37:3)

Joseph was one of Jacob's 12 sons. Joseph was his father's favorite.
Joseph wore a coat that was made of different colors of material.
His brothers wore coats, too, but not as colorful as Joseph's.
The coat showed that Joseph was his father's favorite.
That made his brothers jealous.
"I had a dream," said Joseph. "You were bowing down to me."
That made his brothers angry. "You will not rule over us!" they shouted.
So one day, his brothers took Joseph's colorful coat.
Poor Joseph. He couldn't wear his coat of colors anymore.

Fingerplay

Joseph had a *(pull on one arm of the coat)*

Coat of colors: *(pull on other arm of coat)*

Red and blue, *(extend one arm, palm up)*

Yellow, green. *(extend other arm, palm up)*

What a handsome jacket, *(hug self)*

Joseph's coat of colors: *(turn all the way around)*

Red and blue, *(extend one arm, palm up)*

Yellow, green. *(extend other arm, palm up)*

Pharaoh's Dream

Genesis 41

BIBLE VERSE

"Pharaoh said to Joseph, 'I had a dream.'" (Genesis 41:15)

Pharaoh was sleeping. He had a dream about seven thin cows eating seven fat cows.

Then Pharaoh fell asleep again and had another dream.

This time seven heads of thin grain ate seven heads of fat grain.

Pharaoh asked magicians what his dream meant, but they didn't know.

Pharaoh asked wise men what his dream meant, but they didn't know.

Pharaoh asked Joseph what his dream meant, and God helped Joseph.

"The dreams are one in the same," said Joseph. "There will be seven years when people have enough food. Then there will be seven years when people will not have enough food."

Pharaoh appointed men to store food so his people would not be hungry.

Fingerplay

Pharaoh's sleeping; *(palms together, cheek resting on hands)*

Pharaoh's dreaming. *(point to head)*

He woke up: *(stretch arms outward)*

What a dream! *(hands up, palms out, in surprise)*

"Joseph, can you tell me, *(shrug shoulders, palms upward)*

Tell me what my dream means?" *(fist on chin, look up, thinking)*

"Yes, I can. *(nod head yes)*

If God helps." *(point up)*

Joseph in Egypt

Genesis 42

Jacob told his sons to go to Egypt to buy grain.

Ten sons went to Egypt, but the youngest brother, Benjamin, stayed home with Jacob.

Joseph was the one who sold grain in Egypt. When his brothers arrived, they did not know him. They bowed down to him. Joseph pretended not to know his brothers.

"Where do you come from?" asked Joseph, even though he knew the answer.

"We come from Canaan to buy food," said his brothers.

"You are spies!" said Joseph. "Go home and bring me your youngest brother."

Joseph kept Simeon with him. He gave grain to his brothers to bring home.

They would go home and get Benjamin. Joseph didn't tell his brothers who he was—not yet.

Fingerplay

Help us, Joseph. *(arms extended; palms upward)*

We are hungry. *(hand on stomach)*

You have food; *(point)*

We do not. *(point to self, shake head no)*

Look! They are your brothers. *(point to a child)*

Look! They are your brothers. *(point to another child)*

Come and eat; *(wave to self)*

Come and eat. *(hand to mouth)*

Baby Moses

Exodus 2

Pharaoh's daughter went to bathe in the Nile River.
She saw a basket floating on the river. She asked her maid to get the basket.
Pharaoh's daughter opened the basket. She saw a baby boy!
He was crying. Poor little baby boy, thought Pharaoh's daughter. He must be hungry.
The maid went to get a woman to feed him.
She didn't know it, but the woman was the baby's mother.
"Take this baby and feed him," said Pharaoh's daughter. "I will pay you."
So the baby's mother was able to raise her son until he grew older.
Then she took him to the Pharaoh's daughter, who named him Moses.
Then Moses became the son of the Pharaoh's daughter.

BIBLE VERSE

"He was crying, and she felt sorry for him." (Exodus 2:6)

Fingerplay

Pharaoh's daughter (*hands on head to show headdress*)

Saw a baby (*clasp elbows and rock baby*)

In the Nile, (*point down*)

River Nile. (*show curving motion with hand for waves of water*)

What a fine boy baby! (*clasp elbows and rock baby*)

I will call him Moses. (*point self*)

Moses mine; (*rock baby*)

Moses mine. (*look at baby as you bring arms close to chest*)

Moses in Midian

Exodus 2

Moses grew up and went to live in Midian. He sat down by a well.
Seven sisters came to the well to get water for their sheep.
While they were getting water, some shepherds came to the well.
The shepherds started to drive away the sisters' sheep.
Moses stopped the shepherds from taking the sheep.
Then he got water for the sheep to drink.
The sisters told their father what Moses had done.
Their father asked Moses to eat with them.
Their father asked Moses to stay with them.
Then their father asked Moses to marry his daughter, Zipporah.

Fingerplay

Moses helped them (*pretend to pull jar on rope up from well*)

To get water (*pretend to hold a jar with both hands*)

For their sheep, (*sweep pointer finger at "sheep"*)

For their sheep. (*pour jar of water into trough*)

"We thank you for helping," (*shake hands with neighbor*)

People said to Moses. (*shake hands with another neighbor*)

"Come with us. (*wave to self*)

Stay with us." (*wave to self*)

God Called Moses

Exodus 3–4

Moses led his flock of sheep to the mountain of God. There, Moses saw a bush on fire.

God called to Moses from within the bush.

"I have seen my people suffer," God said to Moses. "Go to Pharaoh and bring my people out of Egypt."

"Who am I to go to Pharaoh?" asked Moses.

"I will be with you," said God.

"What if they don't listen to me?" asked Moses.

"Throw down your cane," said God.

Moses threw down his cane and God turned it into a snake.

"Take it by the tail," said God.

Moses picked up the snake and it turned back into a cane.

Fingerplay

Moses saw a *(hand above eyes, palm down)*

Fire burning *(flutter fingers for fire)*

On a bush, *(make circular motion)*

Burning bush. *(continue to flutter fingers)*

God was calling Moses; *(cup hands near mouth)*

God was calling Moses: *(cup hands near mouth)*

"Throw your cane. *(pretend to throw down cane and point to a "snake")*

Pick it up." *(cautiously pick up the pretend snake/cane)*

Brother Aaron

Exodus 4–5

"**P**lease let someone else go to Pharaoh," said Moses.

"What about your brother, Aaron?" asked God.

Aaron met Moses near the mountain of God.

Moses told Aaron about talking to Pharaoh.

Moses told Aaron how God made the cane turn into a snake.

Moses and Aaron had a meeting with the elders.

Aaron told the elders what Moses had said.

Moses threw down his cane and picked up a snake.

The elders believed the Lord had sent them.

Then Moses and Aaron went to talk to Pharaoh.

Fingerplay

Moses asked his *(one hand out, palm up)*

Brother Aaron, *(other hand out, palm up)*

"Please help me." *(hands clasped)*

"Yes, I will." *(nod head yes; point to self)*

We will go to Pharaoh; *(hold hand with neighbor)*

We will go to Pharaoh. *(walk in place)*

We will talk *(cup hand near mouth)*

To Pharaoh. *(hands on head to show headdress)*

Let My People Go!

Exodus 5

Aaron and Moses talked to Pharaoh. "God says, 'Let my people go.'"
"I do not know the Lord," said Pharaoh. "Why should I obey him?"
Aaron and Moses tried to help the Israelites leave so they could worship God.
"Get back to work!" Pharaoh told the Israelite slaves. "You are lazy."
So Pharaoh gave them more work to do.
Pharaoh had given straw to the Israelite slaves to make bricks.
Now the slaves had to gather straw to make bricks.
They had to work longer days to make bricks.
So the Israelites slaves were angry.
They would not go with Aaron and Moses.

BIBLE VERSE

"The God of Israel says, 'Let my people go.' " (Exodus 5:1)

Fingerplay

"Let my people (*palms upward, extend outward and circle back*)

Go with Moses (*one hand out, palm up*)

And with me," (*point to self*)

Aaron said. (*hands clasped, begging*)

"No, I will not let them," (*shake head no*)

Pharaoh said to Aaron. (*hands on head to show headdress*)

"They will work, (*pound fists in palm*)

Work for me." (*fists to chest*)

Plagues

Exodus 7-10

Moses and Aaron did what God told them to do.

Again, they asked Pharaoh to let the Israelite slaves go.

But Pharaoh did not listen. So God sent frogs:

Frogs in the palace; frogs in the beds; frogs in the bread dough.

"Take away the frogs," said Pharaoh. "I will let the slaves go tomorrow."

So God took away the frogs. When Pharaoh saw the frogs were gone, he changed his mind.

He would not let the slaves go. So God sent more plagues: mosquitoes, flies, sickness, and more.

Even after nine plagues, Pharaoh did not change his mind.

Pharaoh would not let God's people go—not yet.

Fingerplay

Frogs, mosquitoes, (one hand jumps on other open palm)

Flies, and sickness, (pointer and thumb "buzzing" in circles)

Locusts, hail, (hands protecting head)

Then it's dark. (turn around)

Pharaoh was so angry; (stamp foot)

Pharaoh was so angry. (stamp other foot)

God sent plagues; (point up; flutter fingers down)

God sent plagues. (point up; flutter fingers down)

Passover

Exodus 11-12

"**I** will bring one more plague," God told Moses. "Then Pharaoh will let my people go."

At midnight, the Lord struck down the firstborn of the Egyptians.

The Lord passed over the homes of the Israelites.

Many people were crying. Pharaoh asked to see Moses and Aaron.

Pharaoh said, "Leave my people! Go, worship the Lord."

The Israelite slaves had to hurry. They took bread dough before the yeast was added.

Hundreds of thousands of people left Egypt along with sheep and other animals.

Without yeast, they baked bread that did not rise, so it tasted like crackers.

But they were not slaves anymore. They were free!

Fingerplay

God passed over; *(motion hand over head in arch)*

God passed over *(bring hand back, arch in other direction)*

Where we live; *(arms extended, palms outward)*

Where we live. *(point to the ground)*

Celebrate our family; *(turn around)*

Celebrate our family. *(clap three times)*

We have life! *(point to self)*

We have life! *(arms extended)*

Crossing the Red Sea

Exodus 13–14

BIBLE VERSE

Moses said, "Do not be afraid." (Exodus 14:13)

God had led the Israelites out of Egypt.

God was a pillar of cloud during the day so they could see where God led.

God was a pillar of fire at night so they could see where God led.

Again, Pharaoh changed his mind. He wanted the Israelites to work for him.

So Pharaoh followed them. He took an army with horses and chariots to fight the Israelites.

God led the Israelites to the Red Sea.

God told Moses to take his cane and stretch out his hand to divide the waters.

Then the Israelites walked through the sea on dry ground with a wall of water on each side.

Pharaoh and the Egyptians followed. As soon as the Israelites had crossed, God spoke to Moses.

"Stretch your hand over the sea," said God. Moses stretched his hand over the sea.

The water flowed over Pharaoh and the Egyptians.

Fingerplay

People walking; *(walk in place)*

People running *(run in place)*

Far away, *(push air with hand)*

Led by God. *(point up)*

How to cross the Red Sea? *(shrug shoulders, palms up)*

God will part the waters. *(hands together; move hands apart)*

Walk across; *(walk in place)*

Run across. *(run in place)*

Manna From Heaven

Exodus 16

The Israelites traveled in the desert. They complained to Moses and Aaron.

"We had food in Egypt," said the Israelites, "but now we are starving."

The Lord said to Moses, "Bread will rain down from heaven. People should take what they need for just one day."

In the morning, something was on the ground.

"What is it?" the Israelites asked each other.

"It is bread from the Lord," said Moses. "Take what you need just for today, but do not keep it for tomorrow."

Everyone gathered the bread called manna. Some people took just what they needed for today. Some people took more and kept it overnight, but it spoiled.

On the sixth day, they were allowed to gather twice as much manna.

They were allowed to cook it and keep it overnight for the Sabbath. That was the day they worshipped God.

Fingerplay

Everyone was (hands make circular motion)

Getting hungry. (hand on belly)

No more food; (shake head no; keep hand on belly)

No more food. (shake head no)

Then God said to Moses, (point up)

"Food will fall from heaven." (fingers flutter down)

Yum, yum, yum, (rub stomach)

Eat your fill! (hand to mouth)

Moses Prayed

Exodus 17

BIBLE VERSE

"Moses cried out to the Lord, 'What am I to do?'" (Exodus 17:4)

The Israelites traveled from place to place, wherever the Lord led them.

When they camped at Rephidim, there wasn't any water.

The people complained to Moses.

"We are thirsty," they said. "Our children are thirsty. Our animals are thirsty. In Egypt we had water, but here we have no water."

Moses told the Lord what the people had said.

"Ask some elders to go with you to the rock at Horeb," said the Lord.

"Take your cane. I will be with you. Tap the rock with your cane and water will pour out of the rock."

Moses did as the Lord commanded.

Then the people had water to drink.

Fingerplay

Moses prayed hard *(hands together in prayer)*

For some water *(flutter fingers down like rain)*

From a rock, *(pound fist on one palm)*

From a rock. *(pound fist on other palm)*

Everyone was thirsty; *(hand to throat)*

Everyone was thirsty. *(point to one child, then another)*

Drink, drink, drink, *(hand in fist; pretend to drink)*

All you want! *(extend arms in a circle motion)*

The First Commandment

Exodus 19-20

The Israelites camped in the Desert of Sinai.
They camped in front of a mountain called Mount Sinai.
Moses went up the mountain to God.
The Lord said, "Remind the Israelites what I did in Egypt. I carried you on eagles' wings to myself."
The Lord stated his Ten Commandments.
The First Commandment is:
"You shall have no other gods before me."
The Egyptians worshipped many gods,
but the God of Israel is the one true God—and you need no others.

Fingerplay

God gave Moses *(hands extended; palms upward)*

Ten Commandments *(hold up 10 fingers)*

To obey, *(praying hands)*

To obey. *(head bowed)*

I am Lord, your one God; *(point up)*

That's the First Commandment. *(turn around)*

One true God, *(clap once)*

Just one God. *(hold up 1 finger)*

The Second Commandment

Exodus 20

While the Israelites camped in the Desert of Sinai,
Moses was up on the mountain with God.
The Lord said, "Tell the Israelites, if they obey me and keep my covenant, I will make them a holy nation."
The Lord stated his Ten Commandments.
The Second Commandment is:
"You shall not make for yourself an idol."

Fingerplay

"Do not make a *(shake pointer finger)*

Statue of God," *(stand straight and tall; hands at side)*

God commands; *(point up)*

God commands. *(hands on hips)*

That's the next commandment; *(clap twice)*

The Second Commandment. *(turn around)*

One, then two, *(hold up 1 finger, then 2)*

Two commands. *(hold up 2 fingers)*

The Third Commandment

Exodus 20

Moses came down from Mount Sinai.
He went into the Desert of Sinai where the Israelites camped.
Moses told the Israelites what the Lord had said.
Moses reminded the Israelites what God did in Egypt.
He reminded them that God carried them on eagles' wings to himself.
Moses said: "God said, 'If you obey me and keep my covenant, I will make you a holy nation.'"
The Lord stated his Ten Commandments.
The Third Commandment is:
"You shall not misuse the name of the Lord your God."

Fingerplay

Only say the (shake pointer finger in front of you)

Word "God" when you (point up)

Honor him; (praying hands)

Honor him. (praying hands, head down)

That's the Third Commandment; (clap three times)

That's the Third Commandment. (turn around)

One, two, three, (hold up 1, 2, 3 fingers)

Number three. (hold up 3 fingers)

The Fourth Commandment

Exodus 20

God said that people should work for six days
and give the seventh day to the Lord.
The seventh day is the Sabbath day.
On the Sabbath day, people should rest.
God reminded the Israelites that he made the heavens
and the earth in six days and on the seventh he rested.
The Lord rested on the seventh day and told the Israelites
that they should, too. The Lord made the Sabbath day holy.
The Lord stated his Ten Commandments.
The Fourth Commandment is:
"Remember the Sabbath day by keeping it holy."

Fingerplay

Sunday is the *(praying hands)*

Sabbath day, so *(praying hands, head down)*

Remember: *(point to head)*

Rest, rest, rest. *(palms together, cheek resting on hands)*

That's the Fourth Commandment; *(clap four times)*

That's the Fourth Commandment. *(turn around)*

One, two, three, *(hold up 1, 2, 3 fingers)*

Then comes four. *(hold up 4 fingers)*

The Fifth Commandment

Exodus 20

The Israelites wanted to obey the Lord and keep his covenant.
They wanted to be a holy nation.
So Moses went up the mountain to God.
He told the Lord what the people had said.
"The Israelites want to obey you," said Moses. "They want to be a holy nation."
The Lord stated his Ten Commandments.
The Fifth Commandment is:
"Honor your father and your mother."

Fingerplay

God says, "Honor (*praying hands*)

Mom and Dad and (*praying hands; head down*)

Listen well, (*hand to ear*)

And obey." (*nod head yes*)

That's the Fifth Commandment; (*clap five times*)

That's the Fifth Commandment. (*turn around*)

One, two, three, (*hold up 1, 2, 3 fingers*)

four and five. (*hold up 4 and 5 fingers*)

The Sixth Commandment

Exodus 20

BIBLE VERSE

"You shall not commit murder." (Exodus 20:13)

While the Israelites camped in the Desert of Sinai, Moses was up on the mountain.

The Lord said to Moses, "I will come to you in a cloud. The people will hear me talking, but they will not see me. Then they will trust in you."

The Lord stated his Ten Commandments.

The Sixth Commandment is:

"You shall not commit murder."

Fingerplay

"Do not hurt your *(shake pointer finger)*

Friend or brother," *(shake hands with neighbor)*

Says the Lord; *(point up)*

Says the Lord. *(point up)*

That's the Sixth Commandment; *(clap six times)*

That's the Sixth Commandment. *(turn around)*

One, two, three, *(hold up 1, 2, 3 fingers)*

Four, five, six. *(hold up 4, 5, 6 fingers)*

The Seventh Commandment

Exodus 20

While the Israelites camped in the Desert of Sinai, Moses was up on the mountain with God.

The Lord said to Moses, "Get my people ready. On the third day, the Lord will come down and the people will see him.

"Tell them to get ready by washing their clothes.

"Tell them not to go up the mountain on the third day."

The Lord stated his Ten Commandments.

The Seventh Commandment is:

"You shall not commit adultery."

> **BIBLE VERSE**
>
> "You shall not commit adultery." (Exodus 20:14)
>
>

Fingerplay

Show your love by *(one hand on heart)*

Being faithful *(other hand on heart)*

To your friends, *(one hand out, palm up)*

Family. *(other hand out, palm up)*

That's the next commandment; *(clap seven times)*

The Seventh Commandment. *(turn around)*

Now we count *(hold up 1, 2, 3, 4 fingers)*

to seven. *(hold up 5, 6, 7 fingers)*

The Eighth Commandment

Exodus 20

Moses came down from Mount Sinai.
He went into the Desert of Sinai where the Israelites camped.
Moses told the Israelites what the Lord had said.
"Wash your clothes," said Moses. "Get ready for the Lord!"
The Lord stated his Ten Commandments.
The Eighth Commandment is:
"You shall not steal."

Fingerplay

You should not take (grab at air)

What is not yours. (grab at air)

Do not steal! (wave and cross arms in front of you)

Do not steal! (wave and cross arms in front of you)

That's the Eighth Commandment; (clap eight times)

That's the Eighth Commandment. (turn around)

Now one more (hold up 1, 2, 3, 4 fingers)

Equals eight. (hold up 5, 6, 7, 8 fingers)

The Ninth Commandment

Exodus 20

In the camp in the Desert of Sinai, the Israelites awoke on the third morning.
Thunder boomed and lighting flashed. A trumpet blasted.
The Israelites trembled with fear.
Moses led them out of the camp to the foot of the mountain.
Smoke covered Mount Sinai because the Lord came down in fire.
The mountain trembled.
The Lord called Moses to the top of the mountain.
The Lord warned that no one else could come up on the mountain except for Moses and Aaron. So Moses went down the mountain to tell the people.
The Lord spoke his Ten Commandments.
The Ninth Commandment is:
"You shall not give false testimony."

Fingerplay

You should not say *(whisper; cup hand near mouth)*

What is not true. *(shake head no)*

Speak the truth; *(cup hands near mouth)*

Do not lie. *(shake pointer finger)*

That's the Ninth Commandment; *(clap nine times)*

That's the Ninth Commandment. *(turn around)*

Almost done, *(hold up 1, 2, 3, 4, 5 fingers)*

That makes nine. *(hold up 6, 7, 8, 9 fingers)*

The Tenth Commandment

Exodus 20

While God was giving his commandments,
the people stayed at the foot of the mountain.
They trembled with fear.
They were happy God was speaking to Moses
and Moses was speaking to them.
They didn't want God to talk to them directly.
"Do not be afraid," Moses said. "God will help you do the right thing."
But the people still stood back.
Moses walked closer to the dark cloud where God was.
The Lord spoke his Ten Commandments.
The Tenth *(and last)* Commandment is:
"You shall not covet."

Fingerplay

You should not want *(shake head no)*

What your friends have: *(hand over eyes, palm down)*

Toys or clothes, *(pull at your shirt sleeve)*

Or their pets. *(pretend to pet a cat)*

That's the Tenth Commandment. *(clap 10 times)*

That's the Tenth Commandment, *(turn around)*

That makes 10, *(hold up 1, 2, 3, 4, 5 fingers)*

Ten great rules! *(hold up 6, 7, 8, 9, 10 fingers)*

The Ark of the Covenant

Exodus 25

BIBLE VERSE

"I will give you all my commands." (Exodus 25:22)

God gave Moses exact instructions to make an ark.

This ark is not a boat like the ark Noah built for the animals.

This ark is a chest or trunk to carry the stone tablets with the Ten Commandments.

God said, "Use acacia wood. Make it this long and this wide and this high.

"Put gold over it inside and out. Make four gold rings. Put the gold rings on the chest's four feet.

"Make poles out of acacia wood. Put gold on the poles. Put the poles through the rings to carry the chest.

"Make a cover of gold. Make two angels of gold with their wings spread upward."

God was going to give Moses his Testimony to keep in the ark.

Fingerplay

God told Moses, *(point up; then put hand out, palm up)*

"Make a special *(hand to mouth, whispering)*

Container *(hands apart, palms facing each other)*

Called an ark." *(palms facing toward you to form a box)*

A fine chest to carry *(fingers curled, as if carrying)*

All the laws God's given *(hand, circular motion)*

To praise God! *(look up and point)*

To praise God! *(palms up, arms extended)*

The Golden Calf

Exodus 21-32

God explained his laws to Moses, and it took a long time.

So Moses stayed on the mountain a long time.

"Make us a god," the people told Aaron. "We don't know what happened to Moses."

"Give me your gold earrings," said Aaron. "And give me the earrings from your wives and children, too."

Aaron melted the earrings and made them into the shape of a calf.

The next day, the people brought offerings to the golden calf.

But God saw what his people were doing and sent Moses down the mountain.

Moses brought the two stone tablets of God's laws.

When Moses saw the people worshipping the golden calf, he threw down the tablets.

The tablets broke into pieces. Moses took the golden calf and threw it into the fire.

"Come to me," Moses said to the people, "if you are for the Lord."

Fingerplay

Aaron made a (pretend to take off earrings)

Calf of gold and (push air with hands to form calf)

Worshipped it, (bow down; bend elbows and bring hands down)

Worshipped it. (bow down; bend elbows and bring hands down)

"Do not worship gold," said (shake pointer finger)

Moses to the people. (hands on hips)

Worship God! (point up)

Worship God! (raise arms and hands; look up)

Jericho March

Joshua 6

"When the people gave a loud shout, the wall collapsed." (Joshua 6:20)

The Lord told Joshua what to do. Joshua told the people.

On the first day, Joshua walked to the city walls of Jericho.

Joshua brought his men, seven priests holding rams' horns, and the Ark of the Covenant.

They marched around the city walls once.

Everyone was quiet except for the priests, who blew their rams' horns.

Then everyone went back to camp. They did this each day for six days.

On the seventh day, they marched around the city walls six times.

The priests blew their rams' horns. The seventh time around, Joshua told everyone to shout!

Then the walls of Jericho fell down. Joshua and his men could go in the city.

They captured the city of Jericho and devoted the city to the Lord.

Fingerplay

March around the (*feet marching*)

City walls for (*arm extending, palm downward for tall wall*)

Six long days, (*hold up six fingers*)

Blowing horns. (*fist to mouth as if holding a trumpet*)

On the seventh day they (*hold up seven fingers*)

Shout to make the walls fall! (*cup hands near mouth as if shouting*)

Jump for joy! (*jump and clap*)

Walls fall down. (*arms up, palms down; move arms down*)

Strong Samson

Judges 13-16

BIBLE VERSE

"Please, God, strengthen me just once more," prayed Samson. (Judges 16:28)

Samson was so strong, he could not be captured. He won every fight. Samson was in love with a woman named Delilah.

The Philistines were friends of Delilah. The Philistines were enemies of Samson.

The Philistines told Delilah they would give her silver if she helped them capture Samson.

"Tell me your secret," Delilah asked Samson. "What makes you strong?"

"Tie me up with new rope," said Samson. "Then I will be weak."

Delilah tied Samson with new rope, but Samson snapped the ropes.

Delilah kept asking Samson, "What makes you strong?" Finally he told her.

"If my head is shaved, I will become weak."

When Samson was asleep, Delilah asked a man to shave Samson's head.

Then Samson was weak and the Philistines captured him. They put him in prison.

In prison, Samson's hair started to grow. Samson prayed to God to give back his strength.

God granted Samson's prayer.

Fingerplay

Samson was a (move hands over imaginary long hair)

Man of God. (point up)

He was strong, (one hand in fist; bend elbow)

Very strong! (other hand in fist; bend elbow)

Then he had a haircut (move pointer and middle finger in scissors motion)

Making Samson so weak (slump like rag doll)

That he prayed: (praying hands)

"Make me strong!" (hand in fist; bend elbow)

Ruth's Question

Ruth 1

BIBLE VERSE

Ruth said, "Your God will become my God." (Ruth 1:16)

Naomi was filled with sadness when her husband and sons died.
Naomi decided to leave Moab and go back to Judah.
She told her sons' wives to go back to their mothers.
Orpah went back to her mother, but Ruth didn't want to.
"I want to stay with you," Ruth told Naomi.
"Look at Orpah," said Naomi. "She is going back to her mother."
"Don't make me leave you," said Ruth. "Where you go, I will go. Your people will become my people."
So Ruth and Naomi traveled together to Bethlehem in the land of Judah.

Fingerplay

"Can I go, too? (*point to self*)

Please, Naomi," (*kneel down*)

Pleaded Ruth. (*hands clasped, begging*)

"I love you." (*hands over heart*)

"Your way now is my way, (*point to children, then to self*)

And your God is my God." (*point up, then to self*)

"Yes, please come. (*nod head yes*)

You can come." (*wave to self*)

Ruth and Boaz

Ruth 2-4

It was harvest time. Ruth went to work in the fields.
She picked up wheat and barley grain off the ground after it was harvested.
The field where she worked belonged to a godly man named Boaz.
Boaz came to the field where Ruth was working and asked the men about her.
Boaz gave Ruth water to drink and bread to eat.
Boaz told his workers to treat Ruth with kindness. He gave her extra grain to take to Naomi.
Boaz fell in love with Ruth and they were married.
Ruth had a baby named Obed, the grandfather of David, in the line of Jesus.

Fingerplay

Ruth worked in fields *(bend down)*

To have wheat husks *(pretend to pick up husks)*

To grind grain *(grind fist in palm)*

To make bread. *(stirring motion)*

Boaz saw her working *(palm down; hand above eyes)*

And he came to love her. *(hands on heart)*

"Marry me." *(kneel down; clasp hands, pleading)*

"Yes, I will." *(nod head yes)*

Samuel Woke Up

1 Samuel 1–3

BIBLE VERSE

"Speak, Lord, for your servant is listening." (1 Samuel 3:9)

Hannah prayed to the Lord for a child.

"If you give me a son," said Hannah, "I will give him to you."

The Lord granted her prayer. Hannah named her son Samuel.

As soon as Samuel was old enough to stop nursing, Hannah did as she had promised.

She brought Samuel to live with Eli the priest. Samuel would serve the Lord.

One night, the Lord called Samuel. Samuel got up and ran to Eli.

"Here I am," Samuel said. "I did not call you," said Eli.

So Samuel lay down and again the Lord called him.

Samuel got up and ran to Eli.

"Here I am," Samuel said. "I did not call you," said Eli.

This happened once more—then Eli knew the Lord was calling Samuel.

"Next time say, 'Speak, Lord,'" said Eli. That is just what Samuel did!

Fingerplay

Samuel woke up *(stretch arms; eyes closed)*

Hearing God's voice *(open eyes, hand to ear)*

Calling him, *(cup hands near mouth)*

Calling him. *(cup hands near mouth)*

"Father, have you called me? *(gently tap shoulder of child)*

Father, have you called me?" *(shrug shoulders, palms upward)*

"No, not I, *(shake head no)*

It was God!" *(point up)*

David and Goliath

1 Samuel 17

The Philistines and the Israelites were at war.
Goliath was a Philistine and David was an Israelite.
Goliath was nine feet tall. "Choose a man to fight me!" yelled Goliath.
The Israelites ran, but David said he would fight Goliath.
"You are just a boy," said Saul, the king of Israel.
"I have protected my flock of sheep from lions and bears," said David.
They put metal armor and a bronze helmet on David, but it was too heavy.
David took off the armor. He went to the stream and chose five stones.
Then he ran toward Goliath and used his slingshot. A stone hit Goliath's head.
Goliath fell over, dead. That made the Philistines run away!

Fingerplay

David, small, and (palm down, low, at side)

Tall Goliath (palm down, high above head)

Had a fight. (make fists)

Who will win? (shrug shoulders, palms up)

David fought the giant (palm down, low; then high)

With a rock and slingshot. (circle fist over head as ancient slingshot)

David won! (palm down, low, at side)

David won! (clap three times)

David and Jonathan

1 Samuel 18–20

At first, King Saul liked David. Saul made David a leader in the army.
David lived in Saul's house. David married Saul's daughter, Michal.
Saul had a son named Jonathan.
Jonathan and David liked each other the first time they met.
They became best friends.
Jonathan gave David a gift of his robe, his tunic, and his belt. All was well.
But then the people sang songs praising David.
They said David was a better leader in the army than Saul.
That made Saul jealous. Then Saul hated David. All was not well.
David could not live in Saul's house anymore.
He had to leave quickly. When they said goodbye, Jonathan cried. So did David.
Jonathan helped David escape. Then David was safe.

BIBLE VERSE

"We have sworn friendship with each other," said Jonathan. (1 Samuel 20:42)

Fingerplay

David had a *(palm down, low, at side)*

Very good friend, *(shake hands with your neighbor)*

Jonathan, *(clap three times, once for each syllable)*

Jonathan. *(clap three times)*

They could still be friends, but *(nod head yes)*

They could not be neighbors. *(shake head no)*

David moved *(push air with hand)*

Far away. *(push air with hand)*

Young Solomon

1 Kings 3

David had a son named Solomon.

Solomon grew up and married the daughter of the Pharaoh of Egypt.

In a dream, the Lord appeared to Solomon.

"What do you want me to give you?" asked the Lord.

"How kind, O Lord my God," said Solomon.

"I am so young—I do not know how to be a king. Please give me a discerning heart so I can be a good king.

"Help me know what is right and what is wrong."

God was happy with Solomon's answer. "You did not ask for gold or for a long life.

"I will give what you asked for, a wise and discerning heart. I will give you what did not ask for, gold and honor.

"If you keep my commands, I will give you a long life. You will be a great king!"

Then Solomon woke up and realized he was dreaming, but his dream came true.

Fingerplay

Solomon asked *(clasp hands)*

God for wisdom, *(point up, then to head)*

Not for gold, *(shake head no)*

Not for jewels. *(wag pointer finger)*

"I shall give you all things: *(palms up, arms extended)*

Wisdom, jewels and riches," *(point to head, to ring finger, sweep thumb over fingers)*

Said the Lord, *(point up)*

Said the Lord. *(palms up, arms extended)*

Solomon's Heart

1 Kings 7-11

It took Solomon 20 years to build a royal palace and a temple of the Lord. The huge palace was made of cedar beams and cut stones.

Solomon's throne was made of gold and ivory. He drank from goblets made of gold.

The Temple was also filled with gold: a golden altar, golden lampstands, and golden bowls.

When the Temple was complete, the Lord appeared to Solomon.

"My heart will always be here," said the Lord.

Solomon had many wives who were not Israelites. His wives turned his heart to worship their gods.

The Lord was angry because Solomon's heart turned away from the one true God.

BIBLE VERSE

Solomon's heart "had turned away from the Lord." (1 Kings 11:9)

Fingerplay

Solomon had (*palms upward*)

Many riches (*move palms out and circle back*)

Ivory, gold, (*point to ring finger*)

Wisdom, too. (*point to head*)

He began to worship (*praying hands*)

In a pagan temple. (*stand on one foot, then the other*)

No, no, no! (*shake head no; stamp foot three times*)

Worship God! (*point up*)

Queen Esther

Esther 1-9

King Xerxes married Esther, a beautiful young woman.

Haman worked for King Xerxes. Haman wanted to kill all the Jews.

The king didn't know Esther was a Jew.

Esther went to the king when he was sitting on his throne holding his golden scepter.

"What can I give you?" asked King Xerxes. "I will give you half of my kingdom if you want it."

But all Esther asked for was if Haman could eat dinner with them.

Haman came to dinner. There, King Xerxes asked Esther, "What can I give you? I will give you half of my kingdom if you want it."

"If it pleases you," said Esther, "I ask for my life and the life of my people, the Jews."

"Who is planning to kill you?" asked the king.

"It is Haman," said Esther.

Haman was punished, and the king saved Esther and her people, the Jews.

Fingerplay

See Queen Esther; *(point in the distance)*

See Queen Esther: *(cup both hands on head like crown)*

Pretty Queen, *(hand, circular motion over face; smile)*

And smart, too. *(point to head)*

Esther asked the king, "Please, *(kneel)*

Can you save my people?" *(hands clasped, begging)*

The king said, *(cup both hands on head like crown)*

"Yes, I can." *(nod head yes)*

Job Loved God

Job 1 and 42

Job did what was good. He turned away from evil.

Job had seven sons and three daughters.

He owned thousands of sheep, camels, oxen, and donkeys.

One day, the devil presented himself before the Lord.

"Have you seen my servant, Job?" the Lord asked the devil. "He is a godly man."

"If you take away everything Job has," said the devil, "he will not praise you."

"You can do anything, but do not harm Job," the Lord said to the devil.

Job's oxen, donkeys, and camels were stolen.

The house fell in on Job's sons and daughters.

Job said, "The Lord gave and the Lord has taken away." He praised the name of the Lord.

Job was patient. But this was just the first test.

Fingerplay

Job, a good man (hold out one fist in strength)

Whose faith was strong, (hold out other fist in strength)

Prayed to God (praying hands)

And loved God. (hands on heart)

Everything was taken, (hands, grabbing motion)

But Job prayed and thanked God. (praying hands, head down)

This was just (shake head no)

The first test. (hold one finger up)

God Loved Job

Job 1–42

Job was sad. He had lost his sons and daughters, and his oxen, donkeys, and camels.

A second time, the devil presented himself before the Lord.

"Have you seen my servant, Job?" the Lord asked the devil. "He still praises me even with all you took from him."

"I did not touch Job," said the devil. "If I make Job ill, he will not praise you."

"You can do anything, but do not kill Job," the Lord said to the devil.

So the devil made Job sick.

Three of Job's friends tried to help him.

"Ask God for forgiveness," they said.

So Job asked God for forgiveness.

Job didn't understand why he was hurting, but he was humble.

And in the end, God gave Job twice as much as he had before.

Fingerplay

Job had loved God *(arms extended upward)*

With all his heart, *(hands on heart)*

Very great *(hands far apart, palms inward)*

Was his love. *(hands on heart)*

God said I will bless you *(place hand on forehead)*

Because you have been sad. *(pointer finger below eye for tear)*

God loved Job; *(hands on heart)*

God loves you! *(point to children)*

God's Word

Psalm 119

Reading the Bible is like turning on a light in a dark room.
It's like having a flashlight when you're outside at night.
Then you can see the path and where you should walk.
Promise to follow the laws written in the Bible.
Praise the Lord!
Ask the Lord to teach you his laws and help you to understand them.
Ask him to help you to follow them.
And to keep people away who make you turn away from his laws.
God wants you to serve him and do things that make him smile.
He wants you to love his commands more than gold.

Fingerplay

God's Word is like *(point up)*

Light in darkness *(hand in fist, then open up)*

For our feet, *(point fist at your feet, then open)*

For our feet. *(point finger to feet)*

A light in the darkness, *(point fist ahead and open up)*

We can see our steps so *(walk in place, make fist and open up)*

We won't fall, *(shake head no, and keep walking in place)*

We won't fall. *(shake head no)*

Daniel in the Lions' Den

Daniel 6

King Darius signed a new law.

"If anyone prays to any god or person except me," the law stated, "they will be thrown in the lions' den."

A group of men found Daniel praying to God, so they threw Daniel into the lions' den.

They rolled a stone over the lions' den so Daniel couldn't escape.

Even though King Darius liked Daniel, he said that the law must be obeyed.

But King Darius could not sleep that night. He checked on Daniel in the morning.

"Has your God protected you from the lions?" asked the king.

"My God has protected me," said Daniel. "The lions have not hurt me."

The king was overjoyed and gave the orders to let Daniel out of the lions' den.

Then King Darius wrote a new law saying everyone must honor the God of Daniel.

Fingerplay

Guards threw Daniel (*two hands in fists, elbows bent, then straight*)

to the lions. (*fingers curled like big claws*)

Daniel prayed, (*hands together praying*)

Daniel prayed: (*hands together praying, head down*)

"Lions, do not eat me." (*fingers curled like big claws; point to self*)

Lions did not eat him. (*fingers curled like big claws; shake head no*)

Praise to God! (*palms outward, arms extended upward*)

Praise to God! (*palms outward, arms extended even higher; look up*)

Jonah and the Whale

Jonah 1-4

BIBLE VERSE

"From inside of the fish Jonah prayed to the Lord." (Jonah 2:1)

God asked Jonah to go to Nineveh. The people in Nineveh were not obeying God.

But Jonah did not want to go to Nineveh. So he went on a big boat.

The boat was going to sink in a storm. The sailors knew Jonah disobeyed God. So they threw Jonah overboard. Then the boat didn't sink.

But Jonah was swallowed by a whale. He stayed in the whale for three days. Then the whale spit him out onto dry land.

God asked Jonah to go to Nineveh. This time Jonah went.

He told the people to obey God, and they did!

Fingerplay

Once a great whale (*palms inward, hands wide apart*)

Swallowed Jonah (*hands to throat*)

For three days (*hold up three fingers*)

And three nights. (*hold up three fingers*)

Jonah did not taste good (*shake head no*)

So the whale spit Jonah (*touch fingertips to mouth, then push away*)

On dry land, (*point down*)

On dry land. (*point down*)

The Angel Gabriel

Luke 1

God sent an angel named Gabriel to talk to Mary.
"Greetings!" said Gabriel. "The Lord is with you."
Mary was afraid.
"Do not be afraid," said the angel. "You will have a baby and name him Jesus."
"How can this be?" asked Mary.
"Nothing is impossible with God," said Gabriel.

Fingerplay

An angel came to *(clasp hands; look up)*

Visit Mary, *(clasp hands; look down)*

"Do not fear *(sweep pointer finger back and forth)*

God loves you! *(hands on heart; point to children)*

You will have a baby *(clasp elbows to hold baby)*

Whom you will call Jesus." *(pretend to rock a baby)*

Praise the Lord! *(palms outward, arms extended upward)*

Praise the Lord! *(look up; extend arms even higher)*

Mary's Ride

Matthew 1; Luke 2

Caesar Augustus issued a decree.

He wanted a census to be taken of the Roman world.

That meant they would count each person to see how many people lived there.

Each family had to register in their own town.

So Mary rode on a donkey, and Joseph walked from Nazareth to Bethlehem.

They needed to be counted with Joseph's family in the line of David.

It was a long way from Nazareth to Bethlehem, and Mary was going to have a baby.

Fingerplay

Mary rode up *(pretend to hold reins to ride)*

On a donkey; *(bend knees slightly up and down)*

Joseph walked. *(walk in place)*

Bethlehem *(clap three times)*

Was so very crowded. *(gently stand shoulder to shoulder with a child)*

There was no more room in *(shake head no)*

Bethlehem, *(clap three times)*

Bethlehem! *(clap three times)*

In a Stable

Matthew 1; Luke 2

There were so many people in Bethlehem for the census.
Everyone needed a place to stay.
By the time Mary and Joseph arrived,
there was no more room in the inn.
So they had to sleep with the animals.
It was time for Mary's baby to be born.
She gave birth to a baby boy, her firstborn son.
Mary wrapped her baby in swaddling cloth,
and she placed him in a manger.

Fingerplay

Mary gave birth *(two hands on tummy)*

In a stable *(palms up, out, and circle back)*

To a boy, *(clasp elbows to hold baby)*

Baby boy. *(clasp elbows and rock baby)*

Wrapped him in a blanket, *(one hand holding, other circling to wrap)*

Laid him a manger *(palms up; put baby down)*

On the hay *(kneel down, praying hands)*

By the lambs. *(palms down, curled, by forehead for sheep ears)*

Christ Is Born!

Luke 2

Near where Mary had her baby, shepherds watched their sheep at night. An angel appeared to the shepherds, and they were afraid.

"Do not be afraid," said the angel. "I bring you good news that will cause great joy!

You will find a baby, wrapped in swaddling cloth, lying in a manger."

More angels came and said, "Glory to God and peace on earth."

When the angels left, the shepherds said, "Let's go to Bethlehem and see the baby."

They hurried! And they found Mary, Joseph, and the baby in the manger. Then they spread the word about what they had heard and seen.

Fingerplay

Angels came to (clasp hands; look up)

Tell the shepherds, (point far away)

"I bring joy! (clap three times)

Christ is born!" (clasp elbows and rock baby)

"Let's go see the baby," (wave to self)

Said the happy shepherds. (point to the corners of your smile)

"Then let's tell (cup hands around mouth)

Everyone." (hands out and circle back)

Wise Men

Matthew 2

Wise men followed a star in the east. As they traveled, they asked about the newborn baby.

"We want to worship him," said the wise men.

But King Herod was not happy about the newborn baby.

People were calling the baby the "king of the Jews."

King Herod did not want a new king. "I am the king," said King Herod.

So King Herod talked to the wise men. He told them a lie:

"I want to worship the baby, too. When you find him, tell me where he is."

The wise men found Mary and her baby. Then bowed down and worshipped the baby.

They gave gifts of gold, frankincense, and myrrh.

But the wise men did not tell King Herod where the baby was.

They were warned about his lie in a dream. So they traveled to their country another way.

Fingerplay

Three wise men came (*hold up three fingers*)

From the east, they (*point to the east*)

Saw a star (*palm down above eyes, looking*)

Shine so bright! (*open hands and wiggle fingers*)

Following the star they (*point to star*)

Found the baby Jesus, (*elbows clasped to rock baby*)

Then each man (*hold up one, two, then three fingers*)

Gave a gift. (*palms up and outward*)

Just Like Me!

Luke 2

BIBLE VERSE

"He was named Jesus." (Luke 2:21)

Just like you, Jesus was once a baby. Your parents gave you a name.
When Jesus was eight days old, his parents gave him a name.
The angel had told Mary to name her baby "Jesus."
So they named the baby Jesus.
Then Mary and Joseph went to the Temple to present Jesus to the Lord.
There was a man in the Temple named Simeon who took Jesus in his arms.
"Sovereign Lord," said Simeon, "you have kept your promise."
There was an old woman there named Anna.
When she saw Jesus, Anna gave thanks to God.

Fingerplay

Baby Jesus, (clasp elbows and look at baby)

Baby Jesus, (pretend to rock a baby)

Little boy, (tiptoe in place)

Little boy! (tiptoe in place)

Jesus was a baby, (crouch down)

A tiny, little baby; (put hands on head)

Then he grew, (stand up)

Just like you! (point to children)

Hide and Seek

Luke 2

Every year Jesus and his family traveled to Jerusalem.

They celebrated the Jewish holy day called Passover.

When Jesus was 12 years old, he stayed in Jerusalem after Passover.

Mary and Joseph didn't realize that Jesus was not with them on the trip home.

So they went back to Jerusalem to find Jesus.

After three days, they found Jesus in the Temple asking questions.

"We were looking for you," said Mary. "We were worried."

"Why were you looking for me?" asked Jesus. "Didn't you know I'd be in the Temple, which is my Father's house?"

His parents did not understand what he meant.

Jesus went with his parents back home to Nazareth.

He grew in wisdom and favor with God and men.

Fingerplay

Where is Jesus? *(shrug shoulders)*

Where is Jesus? *(palms up)*

There he is! *(point)*

There he is! *(point)*

"Jesus, we were worried. *(hands on hips)*

We were looking for you." *(palm down, above eyes, looking)*

Praise the Lord! *(arms up; look up)*

He's not lost. *(shake head no)*

John the Baptist

Matthew 3; Mark 1; Luke 3; John 1

BIBLE VERSE

"Prepare the way for the Lord." (Matthew 3:3)

A man named John was called "John the Baptist."

He ate locusts and honey and wore clothes of camels' hair.

He told people that Jesus was coming. "Repent!" said John.

John baptized people in the Jordan River.

Jesus came to the Jordan River to be baptized. But John said, "You should baptize me."

"No," said Jesus. "I need you to baptize me."

Then John agreed, and he baptized Jesus in the Jordan River.

Then a dove, the Spirit of God, landed on Jesus' shoulder.

A voice from heaven said, "This is my Son, whom I love."

Fingerplay

John said, "Look, now, *(palm down above eyes, looking)*

Look who's coming: *(point)*

Jesus Christ! *(jump and point)*

See him come?" *(palm down above eyes, looking)*

Come down to the river; *(wave to self)*

Come down to the river. *(make a curvy motion with hand)*

Baptize me; *(hands on head, bend down)*

Wash me clean. *(smooth hands over hair)*

Sermon on the Mount

Matthew 5

Jesus saw crowds of people. He walked up a mountainside and sat down.
His disciples walked up the mountainside, too.
Jesus began to teach them.
"Blessed are the poor in spirit," said Jesus. "Theirs is the kingdom of heaven."
"Blessed are those who are hungry," said Jesus, "for they will be filled."
Jesus continued to teach this way.
He ended with, "Rejoice and be glad!"

Fingerplay

"Bless-ed are those (look down; hands clasped)

Who are hungry," (hand on belly)

Jesus said. (cup hands near mouth)

Jesus preached. (arms extended)

You will not be hungry; (shake head no)

You will not be hungry. (sweep pointer finger left and right)

You will eat (bring hand to mouth)

'Till you're full. (hand on stomach; smile)

Our Father

Matthew 6; Luke 11

Jesus told people how not to pray.
"Do not pray in the temple so people will see you.
"Do not pray on the street so people will see you."
Then Jesus told people how to pray.
"When you pray, go into a room and close the door.
"Pray in secret, and do not go on and on and on.
"Your father knows what you need before you ask him."
Then he said a prayer. It starts, "Our Father in heaven, hallowed be your name."

BIBLE VERSE

"This is how you should pray." (Matthew 6:9)

Fingerplay

Jesus said, "Let's *(cup hands near mouth)*

Pray this way. Say *(praying hands)*

'Our father *(point up)*

In heaven, *(point up)*

Hallowed be thy name,' say, *(praying hands)*

'Our father in heaven.'" *(point up)*

Jesus said, *(kneel)*

"Pray this way." *(praying hands)*

Jesus Heals

Matthew 8; Mark 1; Luke 5

BIBLE VERSE

"Jesus reached out his hand and touched the man." (Matthew 8:3)

Jesus came down from the mountainside.
Large crowds of people followed him.
A very sick man knelt down before Jesus.
"Lord, would you make me well?" asked the man.
"Yes, I will make you well," said Jesus. "Be well!" And the man was well. He was not sick anymore!
"Do not tell anyone," said Jesus. "But go to the priest and thank God."

Fingerplay

A sick man was *(hunch over)*

Touched by Jesus *(touch someone gently on the shoulder)*

And was healed. *(stand up straight and tall)*

Praise the Lord! *(palms up; arms extended)*

He was very happy *(point to smiling mouth)*

So he told the priest how *(cup hands to mouth)*

Jesus heels. *(touch someone gently on the shoulder)*

Miracles! *(fingers spread apart; look up)*

Weed and Flower

Matthew 13

Jesus sat by the lake. Large crowds of people gathered around him.
There were so many people. Jesus got into a boat.
People stood on the shore listening.
Jesus told them stories called parables.
"The kingdom of heaven is like a farmer who planted wheat seeds in a field," said Jesus.
"While the farmer was sleeping, an enemy came and planted weeds. The wheat grew, but so did the weeds.
"The farmer's helpers asked, 'Should we pull the weeds?'
"'No,' said the farmer. 'They are growing so close together, you will pull up the wheat, too.
"Let them both grow. Then it will be easier to pull the weeds, and then harvest the wheat.'"

Fingerplay

Good and bad (*turn one hand over to show palm; then the other*)

Are side by side (*palms together, side by side*)

In this world, (*point down*)

In this world. (*curve hands as if holding a ball*)

God will separate them (*bring palms together, then apart*)

Like a weed and flower. (*pretend to pick weed and flower*)

God will help (*hands in fists*)

Flowers bloom! (*open fists*)

So Big!

Matthew 13; Mark 4; Luke 13

The people wanted to hear more, so Jesus told more parables. People listened from the shoreline. Jesus preached from the boat. One parable was about a tiny mustard seed.

"The kingdom of heaven is like a mustard seed," said Jesus.

"It is one of the smallest seeds, but it grows so big! It is one of the largest plants. It is so large, birds sit in its branches."

Fingerplay

Mustard seeds are *(look at cupped hand as if it holds seeds)*

Very tiny, *(pick a seed from cupped hand with pointer finger and thumb)*

But they grow *(palm downward, hand above your head, looking)*

Very tall. *(continue looking gradually higher)*

Seeds are like God's kingdom, *(pointer finger and thumb together holding seed)*

Which can grow in your heart. *(hands over heart)*

It can grow *(palm downward, low to ground)*

Very tall. *(palm downward, hand above head)*

Bread Dough

Matthew 13; Luke 13

BIBLE VERSE

"The kingdom of heaven is like yeast ...mixed into flour." (Matthew 13:33)

The people wanted to hear more, so Jesus told more parables. The people listened from the shoreline. Jesus preached from the boat. One parable was about yeast, which is used to make bread dough rise. "The kingdom of heaven is like bread dough," said Jesus. "Mix yeast and water with a large amount of flour to make bread dough. The yeast will make the bread dough rise."

Fingerplay

What is like yeast (shrug shoulders, palms up)

Mixed with flour (stirring motion)

Into dough, (fingers curved in shape of ball)

Into dough? (pat ball of dough)

Yeast will make bread dough rise (palm downward, move hand higher)

Like the kingdom of God: (point up)

It starts small, (crouch down)

Then it grows. (stand up)

Buried Treasure

Matthew 13

Jesus got out of the boat where he was preaching.
He left the crowds of people at the shoreline and went into the house.
His disciples wanted to hear more, so Jesus told more parables.
"The kingdom of heaven is like treasure buried in a field," said Jesus.
"When a man found the treasure, he hid it again. But the man was not happy or joyful. So he sold all he had.
"Then the man bought the field."

Fingerplay

Buried treasure, *(hands in digging motion)*

Buried treasure *(hands in digging motion)*

In the ground *(point down)*

In a field. *(palms down, out, then circle back)*

Sell all your possessions; *(palms up, out, in giving motion)*

Sell all your possessions. *(palms up, out, in giving motion)*

Buy the field! *(palms down, out, then circle back)*

Treasure's mine. *(hug self)*

Two Fish

Matthew 14; Mark 6; Luke 9; John 6

BIBLE VERSE

"Looking up to heaven, he gave thanks and broke the loaves." (Matthew 14:19)

Jesus saw a large crowd of people and he wanted to help them.

He took time to heal anyone who was sick.

"It's getting late," the disciples told Jesus. "Send these people away so they can buy food to eat."

"They don't need to go," said Jesus. "You will feed them."

"We only have five loaves and two fish," said the disciples.

"Bring them to me," said Jesus.

He looked up to heaven and gave thanks. Then he gave the loaves and fish to the disciples.

The disciples gave the loaves and fish to the people.

There was enough for everyone to eat, and they had 12 basketfuls left over!

Fingerplay

Two fish and five *(hold up two fingers, then five)*

Barley loaves can *(hands apart, palms inward to show loaf)*

Feed a crowd, *(hand to mouth)*

Feed a crowd. *(hand to mouth)*

Jesus fed 5,000 *(hands together, then far apart)*

Fish and bread for supper. *(hand to mouth)*

Miracles! *(palms outward, near face)*

Miracles! *(raise hands to sky)*

Money for the King

Matthew 18

Jesus told another parable. The kingdom of heaven is like a king and his servants.

One servant owed a lot of money, but he couldn't pay.

"Sell everything you have so you can pay me," said the king.

"Be patient with me," begged the servant, "and I will pay you back."

The king felt sorry for the man.

"I forgive your debt. You don't have to pay me—you may go."

This is how God wants us to forgive each other.

Fingerplay

Once a servant *(hands clasped, head down)*

Owed some money *(palm up, bring thumb across fingers)*

To the king, *(cup hands on head like a crown)*

To the king. *(cup hands on head like a crown)*

"Give me time, I'll pay you," *(hands clasped, begging)*

Begged the lowly servant. *(kneel down)*

"Never mind," *(elbow bent, palm outward, then down)*

Said the king. *(cup hands on head like a crown)*

Lost and Found

Luke 15

The people wanted to hear more, so Jesus told more parables. One parable was about a lost coin.

"What if a woman has 10 silver coins," said Jesus, "but she loses one. Don't you think she would light a lamp to look for it?

"Don't you think she would sweep the house?

"Don't you think she would look until she found it?

"Then when she found her coin, she would call her friends and say, 'Look! I have found my coin!'"

Fingerplay

When a woman (*cross hands over heart*)

Has 10 shining (*show 10 fingers*)

Silver coins; (*hold "coin" in thumb and pointer finger*)

Where is one? (*shrug shoulders, palms up*)

She will get a lantern (*pretend to hold oil lantern*)

And look in the corner (*look on floor in corner*)

For her coin. (*point to coin*)

Here it is! (*hold up coin in thumb and pointer*)

Share

Luke 16

Jesus told more parables. One parable was about a rich man.

There was a rich man who dressed in purple. Only kings and queens or rich people could buy purple clothes.

A poor beggar named Lazarus was at the rich man's gate.

Lazarus was sick and had sores on his body. The dogs licked his sores.

The rich man did not share his food with the poor man.

Lazarus ate food that fell to the floor from the rich man's table.

When Lazarus died, the angels carried him to heaven.

When the rich man died, the angels did not carry him to heaven because he didn't share his food with the poor.

Fingerplay

Once a rich man *(hands on hips, stand tall, nose up in air)*

Saw a poor man *(hand above eyes, palm downward, looking at poor man)*

By his gate, *(elbows out, hands clasped to make "gate")*

By his gate. *(move "gate" back and forth)*

The poor man ate crumbs that *(hand to mouth)*

Fell down from the table *(fingers fluttering down)*

To the floor, *(point down)*

Like a dog. *(get down on all fours)*

Come to Me

Matthew 19; Mark 10; Luke 18

People were bringing babies to Jesus.
They wanted Jesus to touch their babies.
The disciples did not like this.
They told people not to bother Jesus.
But Jesus didn't agree with his disciples.
He liked people bringing their children to him.
"Let the little children come to me," Jesus said.
"If you want to enter the kingdom of God, receive it like a little child."

Fingerplay

Jesus said, "You (point to one child)

Are important! (point to every child)

Come to me; (wave to self)

Come to me!" (wave to self)

Jesus loves the children; (hands outward)

Big and little children, (palm up high, then down low)

Everywhere, (circular motion)

Everywhere. (circular motion)

God's Love

Matthew 20

BIBLE VERSE

"The last will be first."
(Matthew 20:16)

Jesus told more parables. One parable was about a vineyard where grapes are grown.

Early in the morning, a farmer went to find men to work in his vineyard.

"I will pay you $10 for the day," he said.

Later in the morning, the farmer went to find more men to work in his vineyard.

He went out at lunch, and then again in the late afternoon to find more workers.

When it was time to get paid, everyone got paid $10—the workers who came in early morning and the workers who came later.

The workers who had worked all day complained about this. "It's not fair," they said.

But the farmer said, "I want to be generous."

Jesus added, "The last will be first and the first will be last."

Fingerplay

See the vineyard? *(hand above eyes, palm downward, looking)*

See the vineyard? *(point)*

Harvest grapes; *(pretend to pick grapes and put in sack)*

Harvest grapes. *(pretend to pick grapes and put in sack)*

Some of you work all day; *(wipe brow with hand; slouch)*

Some of you work later. *(stand up straight; smile)*

All get paid, *(hand in circular motion for "all")*

Paid the same! *(sweep thumb across fingers)*

The Fig Tree

Matthew 21; Mark 11

BIBLE VERSE

"If you believe,
you will receive."
(Matthew 21:22)

It was early in the morning.
Jesus was traveling and he was hungry.
Jesus saw a fig tree by the road.
He walked up to the tree to pick some figs.
Leaves were growing on the tree, but no figs.
Jesus was still hungry.
Jesus told his disciples, "If you believe, you will receive whatever you ask for in prayer."

Fingerplay

Hungry Jesus (*hand to stomach*)

Saw a fig tree (*hand above eyes, palm downward, looking*)

By the road, (*point down*)

By the road. (*point down*)

It looked strong and healthy (*elbow bent, hand in fist*)

But it yielded no fruit. (*shake head no*)

Ask and you (*hands together in prayer*)

Shall receive. (*bow head*)

The Wedding

Matthew 25

BIBLE VERSE

"Keep watch!"
(Matthew 25:13)

Jesus told another parable. This one was about a wedding.

The kingdom of heaven is like 10 bridesmaids holding lamps.

The bridesmaids went out to meet the bridegroom.

Five of the bridesmaids took extra oil for their lamps.

Five of the bridesmaids did not take extra oil for their lamps.

It was getting late and the bridegroom had not arrived. The lamps needed more oil.

"Give us some of your oil," said the five bridesmaids who did not bring extra oil.

"No, there is not enough," said the five bridesmaids who brought extra oil.

So the five bridesmaids without extra oil went to buy some.

While they were gone, the bridegroom arrived.

He left with the five bridesmaids and their brightly shining lamps.

By the time the others returned, everyone was at the wedding and the door was locked.

They couldn't get in.

Fingerplay

Bridesmaids waiting, *(look at "watch" on wrist)*

Bridesmaids waiting *(hands under cheek, sleeping)*

For the groom, *(palm down, above eyes, looking)*

For the groom. *(palm down, above eyes, looking)*

Five bridesmaids have oil *(hold up five fingers)*

For the lamps they carry. *(pretend to hold oil lantern)*

They can go *(nod head yes)*

To the feast! *(hand to mouth, eating)*

Coins of Gold

Matthew 25

Before a man left on a trip, he gave his servants some money. He gave 5 dollars to one, 2 dollars to another, and 1 dollar to a third. The servant with 5 dollars used it to earn 5 dollars more. The servant with 2 dollars used it to earn 2 dollars more. But the servant with 1 dollar dug a hole and buried it. The man returned. The servant who had received 5 dollars showed that he had earned 5 more. "Well done!" said the man. "I will help you earn even more." The servant who had received 2 dollars showed he had earned 2 more. "Well done!" said the man. "I will help you earn even more." The servant who had received 1 dollar said he had buried it. The man was not very happy. He took back his money and told the servant to leave.

Fingerplay

Once a rich man *(hands on hips, nose up in air)*

Gave three servants *(cup one hand; other giving "coins")*

Coins of gold, *(thumb and pointer finger holding coin)*

Coins of gold. *(thumb and pointer finger holding coin)*

Two worked hard to make more. *(hold up two fingers)*

One was scared and hid his. *(pretend to dig a hole and place coins in)*

Do not fear; *(shake head no)*

Earn some coins. *(cup one hand; other giving "coins")*

Healing Water

John 9

The disciples and Jesus were walking.

They saw a blind man. He was a beggar.

Jesus spit on the ground to make mud. He put mud on the blind man's eyes.

"Go," said Jesus. "Wash in the Pool of Siloam."

So the blind man went to the Pool of Siloam and washed.

Then he could see.

His neighbors asked, "How can you see?"

"Jesus put mud on my eyes," said the man. "He told me to wash in the Pool of Siloam.

"So I washed and then I could see!"

Fingerplay

Once there was a (hands on hips)

Man who could not (sweep pointer finger back and forth)

See at all; (hand over one eye)

He was blind. (hand over other eye)

Jesus healed the man's eyes (take hand away from eyes)

With some mud and water. (rub air in front of eyes in circular motion)

What a great (palms outward, near face)

Miracle! (spread fingers and move wrists; look up)

Jesus Walked

Matthew 14; Mark 6; John 6

Jesus told his disciples to take the boat and leave without him.
He would say goodbye to the crowd of people.
By evening, the disciples had rowed to the middle of the lake.
Jesus was alone on the mountainside, praying.
It was getting dark, but Jesus could see the wind was strong.
He could see it was hard for the disciples to row.
So Jesus went to them, walking on the lake.
The disciples saw Jesus walking on the water and they were frightened. They thought he was a ghost.
"It is I," said Jesus. "Do not be afraid."

Fingerplay

Jesus said, "Go (*push air with hand, palm outward*)

On without me (*turn in a circle*)

In the boat. (*pretend to row boat*)

I will pray. (*praying hands*)

Jesus walked on water; (*walk in place looking around at water*)

Jesus walked on water (*walk in place looking down at water*)

To the boat (*arms crossed over chest*)

In the storm. (*shoulders up, look up*)

Peter Walked

Matthew 14

The wind blew and the waves rocked the boat.
The disciples watched Jesus walk on the water.
But Peter didn't believe it was Jesus.
"If it's you," said Peter, "let me walk on the water."
"Walk to me," said Jesus. So Peter climbed out of the boat onto the water.
He started walking on the water toward Jesus. Then the wind pushed Peter.
He was afraid and started to sink. "Lord, save me!" Peter called to Jesus.
Jesus reached out and caught Peter, and they climbed into the boat.
Then the wind died down.
They crossed the lake, and the boat reached the shore safely.

Fingerplay

"Let me walk, too, (point to self)

On the water," (two fingers walking on other hand)

Peter yelled (cup hands near mouth)

From the boat. (hands together, palms up, cupped to form boat)

But the wind pushed Peter (sway back and forth)

And he started sinking. (bend knees)

"Lord save me!" (hand out, arm extended)

Peter yelled. (cup hands near mouth)

Jesus' Feet

Luke 7; John 12

Jesus was having dinner with Lazarus, Martha, and Mary.
Jesus and Lazarus were sitting at the table. Martha was serving.
Mary took expensive perfume and poured it on Jesus' feet.
Then she wiped his feet with her hair.
The sweet-smelling perfume filled the air in the house.
"Why did she do this?" asked one of the disciples, Judas.
"Leave her alone," said Jesus. "I will not always be with you."

BIBLE VERSE

"She wiped his feet with her hair." (John 12:3)

Fingerplay

Mary knelt down *(kneel)*

On the floor to *(point to floor)*

wash his feet, *(point in front of you)*

wash his feet. *(circular motion in front of you, washing)*

She poured precious oil *(hand in "C" shape, pouring oil)*

On the feet of Jesus. *(pour oil in front of you)*

Then she dried *(circular motion in front of you, drying)*

With her hair! *(hold lock of your own hair)*

The Good Samaritan

Luke 10

"**W**ho is my neighbor?" a man asked Jesus.

To explain the answer to the question, Jesus told a parable.

Once there was a man who was traveling. Robbers hit him and stole his clothes.

A priest saw the man but walked past him.

A Levite saw the man but walked past him.

A Samaritan saw the man and felt sorry for him.

So the Samaritan put bandages where he was hurt, put the man on his donkey, and took him to an inn.

The Samaritan paid the innkeeper to look after the man.

"Which one of these three men was a neighbor to the hurt man?" asked Jesus.

"The one who felt sorry for him," said the man who had asked the question.

"Go and be a good neighbor," said Jesus.

Fingerplay

Once there was a (hunch over)

Man who was hurt (put hand on heart)

By the road, (point down)

By the road. (point down)

One, two men just walked by, (show one finger, then two)

Then a man came and said, (two fingers walking)

"I will help; (point to self)

I will help." (point to self)

Mary Listens

Luke 10

BIBLE VERSE

"Mary has chosen what is better," said Jesus. (Luke 10:42)

Jesus and his disciples were traveling.

A woman named Martha asked them to stay in her home.

Martha had a sister named Mary.

Martha was busy cooking for her guests.

But Mary was not helping. She was just sitting by Jesus, listening to him.

"Lord," said Martha, "my sister has left me to do all the work myself. Tell her to help me!"

"Martha, Martha," said Jesus, "you are worried about too many things. Mary has decided to sit with me. I will not tell her to help you."

Fingerplay

Martha was so *(hands on hips)*

Very busy *(sweeping motion)*

Cooking supper *(stirring motion)*

For her friends. *(palms upward, out, and circle back)*

Mary sat by Jesus *(sit on chair or floor and look up)*

And she listened closely. *(cup hand near ear)*

Martha said, *(shake head no)*

"It's not fair!" *(shake pointer finger)*

Big Harvest

Luke 12

Jesus talked to crowds of people. He told this parable.

One year, a rich farmer's crops grew and grew.

He harvested more grain than ever before!

He had so much, there was nowhere to store the grain.

"I know," said the farmer. "I will tear down my barns and build bigger barns. Then I'll have enough room to store all the grain I harvested. Then I can be lazy."

"Watch out!" said Jesus. "Don't be greedy.

Your life isn't about what you have; it's about honoring God."

Fingerplay

Once there was a *(arms apart, palms inward)*

Big, big harvest. *(spread arms wider apart)*

Farmer said, *(cup hands near mouth)*

"I am rich!" *(point to self)*

All the farmer thought of *(point to head)*

Was his food and money. *(rub stomach; then palm up, rub thumb over fingers)*

He did not *(shake head no)*

Worship God. *(praying hands, close eyes)*

Invitation

Luke 14; Matthew 22

A man was having a big party and invited lots of friends.

When the party was ready, the man sent a servant to his friends' houses.

"Come," said the servant. "Everything is ready for the party."

By then, the friends did not want to go.

"I'm busy," said one friend. "I need to watch over my land."

"I'm busy," said another friend. "I need to watch over my animals."

"I'm busy," said a third friend. "I just got married."

When the servant told his master what his friends had said, the master was angry.

"Go to the streets and bring the poor and homeless," said the master. "Then there will be no room for my friends if they change their minds."

Fingerplay

Once a good man *(hands clasped in prayer)*

Planned a party *(pretend to write on palm)*

At his house: *(wave to self)*

Please come now! *(hands clasped, pleading)*

"I am much too busy." *(shake head no)*

"Then, I'll ask some others," *(wave to self)*

Said the Man, *(cup hands near mouth)*

Said the Man. *(clap three times)*

Prodigal Son

Luke 15

BIBLE VERSE

"He was lost and is found." (Luke 15:32)

Jesus told a parable about two sons.

The younger son asked for money and left home, traveling far away.

He spent all the money his father had given him. He was hungry.

So he went to work feeding pigs. He was so hungry, he wanted to eat the pigs' food.

"I'm going back home," he said.

"I will ask my father to forgive me and take me in."

When the younger son got home, his father was so happy that he had a big party.

The older son was angry.

"I have worked hard for you but you never had a party for me."

"You have always been with me," said his father.

"But your brother was lost and is found."

Fingerplay

Of two sons the (*show two fingers*)

Younger traveled (*two fingers walking*)

Far away, (*push air with hand*)

Far away. (*push air with hand*)

He used all his money. (*show empty hands*)

"I miss home; I'm sorry." (*hands on your head; head down*)

"You were lost! (*palms out, extended in front of you*)

Now you're found!" (*bring hands back and cross arms on chest*)

Zacchaeus

Luke 19

Jesus traveled through Jericho.
A rich man there named Zacchaeus was a tax collector.
Zacchaeus wanted to see Jesus, but he was short.
He couldn't see above the crowd of people.
So Zacchaeus climbed a sycamore-fig tree.
He saw Jesus and Jesus saw him.
"Come down, Zacchaeus," said Jesus. "I must stay at your house today."
Zacchaeus came down from the tree and welcomed Jesus into his home.
But people saw them. "How can Jesus eat with a tax collector?" they asked.
"I am giving half my things to the poor," Zacchaeus told Jesus.
"Today salvation has come to this house," said Jesus.

Fingerplay

Short Zacchaeus, *(palm down, low)*

Small Zacchaeus *(bend knees a little)*

Climbed a tree. *(one arm up, then the other to climb)*

He could see. *(palm down, above eyes, looking)*

Jesus saw Zacchaeus, *(point up to tree)*

"Can we eat together?" *(hand to mouth)*

"Yes, we can. *(nod head yes)*

Come home now." *(wave to self)*

The Widow's Offering

Luke 21; Mark 12

Jesus was in the Temple.
He watched rich people giving money to the Temple.
Jesus watched a woman give two small coins to the Temple.
Jesus knew the woman's husband had died and she was poor.
"This is true," said Jesus. "This poor widow has given more than the rich people.
"They gave money, but have a lot more money.
"She gave all she had to live on."

Fingerplay

Once a widow (*pretend to hold shawl over head*)

Went to Temple. (*two fingers walking*)

She was old; (*hunch shoulders*)

She was poor. (*palms upward*)

She gave all her money, (*pretend to give coin*)

Two small coins of money. (*hold up two fingers*)

That was all (*hunch shoulders*)

That she had. (*palms upward*)

Good Shepherd

John 10

"This is true," said Jesus. "A man who goes into a sheep pen using the gate is the shepherd."

If a man does not enter by the gate but climbs over the fence, he is a robber.

The sheep know their shepherd's voice. The shepherd calls his sheep by their names.

He leads his sheep out of their pen and they follow him because they know his voice.

The sheep will not follow a stranger. The sheep will run from a stranger.

They do not know the stranger's voice.

People didn't understand what Jesus meant, so he explained.

"I am the gate," said Jesus. "Whoever enters through me will be saved. I am the good shepherd. I know my sheep and my sheep know me."

BIBLE VERSE

"I am the good shepherd," said Jesus. (John 10:11)

Fingerplay

A good shepherd *(clasp hands together under chin)*

Knows all his sheep *(sweep pointer finger in front of you)*

In the pen *(palms facing, shoulder-length apart, to show "pen")*

By their names. *(nod head yes)*

Emily and Sarah, *(use names of children in your group)*

Terry, Steve, and Roger *(point to children and say each child's name)*

Are their names, *(move pointer finger on opposite palm)*

Are their names. *(pretend to write on hand)*

The Last Supper

Matthew 26; Mark 14; Luke 22; John 13

BIBLE VERSE

Judas said, "Surely you don't mean me, Rabbi?" (Matthew 26:25)

Jesus celebrated the holy day of Passover with his 12 disciples.

Jesus was sitting at the table with them.

"One of you will betray me," said Jesus.

The disciples were very sad. Each one asked Jesus, "Surely not I, Lord?"

Then Judas said, "Surely you don't mean me, Rabbi?"

"Yes," said Jesus. "It is you."

Then Jesus took a loaf of bread and broke it. He gave thanks and gave pieces of bread to the disciples.

"This bread is my body," said Jesus.

Then Jesus took a drink and gave thanks. He offered the cup to his disciples.

"Take a drink," said Jesus. "Remember me."

Fingerplay

Jesus ate with *(hand to mouth)*

Twelve disciples *(hold up 10 then 2 fingers)*

One last time, *(hold up one finger)*

One last time. *(hold up one finger)*

"This bread is my body; *(hands out, palms up)*

Eat bread to remember. *(hand to mouth; then point to head)*

Eat and drink. *(hand to mouth; fist to mouth for drink)*

Eat and drink." *(hand to mouth; fist to mouth for drink)*

Easter Promise

Matthew 28; Mark 16; Luke 24; John 20

Mary Magdalene and another woman named Mary went to the tomb where Jesus was buried.

An angel rolled back the stone. Then the angel sat on the stone.

The angel was shining brightly and his clothes were as white as snow.

"Do not be afraid," the angel said to the women. "I know you are looking for Jesus.

"He is not here. Come and see. He has risen. Go tell the disciples he has risen.

"Jesus will see you in Galilee."

The women were filled with fear and with joy. They hurried to tell the disciples.

Then they saw Jesus. The women worshipped him.

"Do not be afraid," said Jesus. "Go and tell my brothers I will see them in Galilee."

BIBLE VERSE

"He has risen,"
said the angel.
(Matthew 28:6)

Fingerplay

Easter promise, *(hands clasped)*

Easter promise *(hands clasped; look up)*

Brings new life, *(sweep one hand across air to make arch)*

Brings new life. *(sweep other hand across air to make arch)*

Everything is growing: *(hands, circular motion)*

Flowers of all colors. *(pretend to pick flower)*

Praise to God! *(hop on one foot)*

Praise to God! *(hop on the other foot)*

Happy Easter!

Matthew 28; Mark 16; Luke 24; John 20

Eleven of Jesus' disciples went to Galilee.

Jesus had told them to go there.

He said he would meet them there.

When the disciples saw Jesus, they worshipped him.

But some of the disciples doubted him.

How could this be Jesus? they wondered.

"All authority in heaven and on earth has been given to me," said Jesus.

"Go and make disciples of all nations and teach them everything I have commanded.

"I am with you always to the very end."

Fingerplay

Happy Easter! *(pointer fingers to sides of mouth while smiling)*

Happy Easter! *(clap four times)*

It is spring, *(one palm up, out, and circle back)*

It is spring. *(other palm up, out, and circle back)*

God gives life in springtime; *(squat down)*

God gives life in springtime. *(jump up)*

Sing for joy! *(hands at sides, palms up)*

Sing for joy! *(bring arms up slowly)*

Go Fish!

John 21

The disciples were fishing in the Sea of Galilee.
They did not catch anything that night.
So in the morning, they decided to go fish again.
Jesus stood on the shore, but they did not know it was Jesus.
"Have you caught any fish?" Jesus called out to them.
"No," they answered.
"Throw your net on the right side of the boat," said Jesus. "You will catch some."
They threw the net on the right side of the boat and caught lots of fish!
Then John looked at the man on the shore again. "It is the Lord!" John said.
Simon Peter jumped into the water and swam to shore. The other disciples brought the boat.
They cooked fish over an open fire and ate breakfast with Jesus.

Fingerplay

The disciples (*use two hands to cast fishing net*)

Fished all evening. (*yawn*)

They did not (*shake head no*)

Catch one fish. (*pointer and thumb in circle, zero*)

Jesus told them where to (*hand by mouth*)

Cast their fishing nets out; (*pretend to cast net*)

Then they caught (*pretend to pull up net*)

Lots of fish! (*hands wide apart, palms inward*)

Great Acts

Acts 16

Paul and Silas were in Philippi telling people about Jesus.

Some people didn't like what they were doing. So they put Paul and Silas in jail.

But Paul and Silas kept singing and praising God.

That night there was an earthquake.

The ground shook so much, the doors of the jail opened.

But Paul and Silas didn't leave. They knew the guard would get in trouble if they left.

The guard was so grateful, he asked Paul and Silas how to be saved.

"Believe in the Lord Jesus, and you will be saved," said Paul and Silas.

Then the guard and all his family were baptized.

The guard was filled with joy because he had come to believe in God.

Fingerplay

Silas praised God (*push air up with hands above head in praise*)

And Paul praised God (*push air up with hands above head in praise*)

All the time (*make circle in air with one hand*)

Everywhere. (*palms up, out, then circle back*)

Then there was an earthquake (*move to and fro*)

And the doors were opened! (*grab hold and open "door"*)

But they stayed, (*arms in an "X" across chest*)

Stayed inside. (*crouch down*)

Lots of Letters

Romans-Jude

BIBLE VERSE

"Grace and peace to you." (Romans 1:7)

Have you helped your mom or dad write a letter or email?

Maybe you enclosed or attached a picture you drew or a photograph.

Maybe you told your mom or dad what to write, or maybe you wrote something yourself.

Paul, James, Peter, John, Jude, and others all wrote letters to early churches and new Christians.

The letters offered help in how to trust God.

It told people what to do if there was a problem.

Often, the letters would start out with a greeting.

Your letter or email might begin, "Dear Grandma" or "Dear Grandpa."

A letter from Paul to the Romans began this way:

"Grace and peace to you from God our Father and from the Lord Jesus Christ."

These letters helped early churches grow and become stronger.

Fingerplay

Paul and others (*finger and thumb together*)

All wrote letters (*up and down motion in air, "writing"*)

To Christians (*clap three times*)

To churches. (*hands pointed over head in a steeple*)

We can read their letters (*palms together, closed "book"*)

On the Bible pages (*open palms to read "book"*)

In a book, (*pretend to turn pages*)

Precious book. (*hug self*)

Smile!

2 Corinthians 9

One of the letters Paul wrote to the people in Corinth talked about giving money to the church.

The church helped poor people who needed food, clothes, or a place to sleep. Here are some things Paul said:

If you give just a little, you will get just a little.

If you give a lot, you will get a lot.

Each person should decide how much money to give.

Look into your heart to decide. Don't give with a frown on your face.

Don't give because someone else has forced you to do it.

Give the amount of money you feel good about.

God loves a cheerful giver. Smile when you give!

Fingerplay

Be a very (point to corners of mouth, smiling)

Cheerful giver. (nod and keep smiling)

When you give (palms up, moving outward)

Anything, (fingers spread, hands, circular motion)

Give it with a smile; (pointer fingers at corners of smile)

Smile when you give it. (smile; palms up, moving outward)

God loves joy (point up; then clasp hands)

When you give. (point to two or three children)

THE GIANT

Book of
BIBLE
FINGERPLAYS
for Preschoolers
BY AMY HOUTS

Indexes

Bible Verse
....
Old Testament
....
New Testament
....
Old and New Testaments

Bible Verse

Scripture Index

Old Testament

New Testament

THE **GIANT** BOOK OF BIBLE FINGERPLAYS FOR PRESCHOOLERS

Old Testament

Topic Index

New Testament

Topic Index

THE **GIANT** BOOK OF BIBLE FINGERPLAYS FOR PRESCHOOLERS

Old and New Testaments

Topic Index

More than 200 GIANT-SIZED games to maximize your impact!

The Giant Book of Games for Children's Ministry

This JAM-PACKED, CHOCK-FULL book of more than 200 GIANT-SIZED games will fill your ministry with TONS of fun and laughter! With a variety of games for preschoolers through preteens, you'll find the perfect game for every occasion!

Each of these fun-filled games is tied to a different topic, with a Scripture connection and discussion to help kids understand the Bible point. You'll bring more depth and learning to topics including The Body of Christ, Salvation, Faith, Creation, Fear, Following Jesus, Trust, Forgiveness, Friendship, God's Love, Jesus' Birth and Resurrection, Grace, Prayer, Thankfulness, and so many more!

Every game includes an overview that details the game's energy level, supply level, age level, and preparation needed, so you'll be able to find the best fit for your lesson and time slot. Plus these relational, cooperative games can be used anytime…wherever they fit into your schedule or to fill an on-the-spot need!

Reinforce your lessons with these 200+ must-have games that'll help kids actually remember what they learned!

▶ ISBN 978-1-4707-0424-7 • $29.99

Help kids DIVE DEEPER into what God's Word says about dozens of topics!

The Giant Book of Children's Messages

Packed with more than 100 children's messages, this book will help you encourage kids to explore their faith and praise God. With a variety of devotions for early and upper elementary, you'll find the perfect children's message for every occasion.

Each activity is tied to a different topic, with a Scripture connection and discussion to help kids understand the Bible point. You'll bring more depth to topics including: Choices, Cliques, Faith, Fear, God's Love, Jesus' Miracles, Kindness, Loving Others, Peer Pressure, Self-Image, Sharing Faith, Thankfulness, Teamwork, and so many more!

User-friendly pages include supply lists and a description of preparation needed, so you're able to find the best fit for your lesson and time slot. Plus, these relational, engaging devotions can be used anytime…wherever they fit into your schedule or to fill an on-the-spot need. You'll also find loads of reproducible handouts!

Reinforce your lessons with these 100+ must-have children's messages that'll help kids dive deeper into their faith!

▶ ISBN 978-1-4707-4216-4 • $29.99